HARDROCK

AND

THE ROLLING TIDE

By S.C. Lee

About S.C. Lee

S. C. Lee is an abbreviation for Stonewall Culpepper Lee. Lee is a pen name for the author who started recounting this story five decades ago...was given an advance by a major New York Publisher...but, put the work aside during a life-long career of History and book publishing of over 100 different titles.

THE SCHOOLS HAVE LASTED A HUNDRED YEARS.

THE RIVERS A HUNDRED YEARS ALSO.

THEIR INFLUENCE CONTINUES TO THIS DAY.

SUNLIGHT IN THE HILLS OF APPALACHIA.

SUNSHINE IN TUSCALOOSA.

TABLE OF CONTENTS

1

THE WIDOW
Fired Up

People in Free Fall, Kentucky, believe in Adam and Eve. They also believe in the convicted serpent. Walking alongside a mountain stream that descended as he ascended, a youth nicknamed Hardrock Adams tried hard to avoid shadows, especially those that looked larger. The soft soil felt warm against his bare feet, and he reminded himself that he could always cool them in the gushing mountain stream. He was wearing a light blue shirt above white knee pants, colors that seemed incongruous with his tanned complexion this hot July.

It was a time for daydreams or nightmares, and he remembers dreaming about walking someday beside lakes and oceans wonderfully larger than this creek, daydreaming so much he stepped across a log in the road. Or, that is, a huge log-shaped reptile that raised its head from the angry creek as if to drink him in preference to water. That's also when he began putting whatever daylight he could between himself and his new acquaintance.

Hardrock Adams' errand of mercy was in response to his mother's request to visit a widow who lived up this hollow. So now he raced to the edge of the widow's abandoned water-mill and negotiated a foot-log that crossed the creek to her cabin. From there, rudely unannounced, he barged in, slamming the door hard behind him and his new log-shaped acquaintance.

The widow remained calm as she sat in the shadows in her rocker facing her fireplace fire. She continued blowing gentle puffs of smoke from her pipe toward an empty fireplace.

Her apparent unconcern gave him time to catch his breath before blurting, "Widow, you've – you've got a huge snake out there. I mean out there – in the middle of the road – that looks like a dragon – a terrible big one. So I slammed your door."

He was amazed that she continued killing time by smoking, however, and did so until she spoke with an abruptness seemingly caused in part by choking or smoke. "You shore did that, and I mean to a howdy do."

He was still breathing so hard he sucked in

wood and tobacco smoke himself.

"I was headed up here anyway," he finally heard himself saying. Then he forced a laugh, "I hadn't meant to run."

She removed her pipe and smoke. "A big one, eh?" With this she turned enough to face him instead of the fireplace. "You live in that valley, mister?"

"Yes. I'm Hardrock Adams. I live in the faculty dormitory at the school. My mother teaches there I guess."

"She teaches where? You don't know?"

"Yes."

"And what brings you here?"

"Well, mother sees you come down every Saturday."

The widow stiffened slightly. "Oh?"

"Yes'm. When you come down to the swinging bridge between our house and where your creek heads into the river, she sees you going to the store."

"She sees me – oh I see."

"Yes. Going to the store."

The widow gradually lowered her pipe and rested it on the hearth. Next from shadows on the other side of her rocker she found a cane that eventually helped her to her feet. Then for some reason, perhaps celebrating, she laughed briefly. "I ain't sure why, but you keep looking to me like a little God or angel, son. Which is it?" Without warning she leaned over, selected a broom straw from a pint jar near her chair, and lit the straw in her fire. Then ignoring him she entered shadows deeper in the room, finally shoving the straw down a smoky globe and lighting a table lamp. After this she returned eventually to the fireplace and tossed in the lighted straw before, with the help of her crutch, turning to face him again. "I never seen a prettier child. And you a boy too."

"Well I…"

"I'll open the door and make sure."

"You don't mean open the door, widow? I closed it good."

She smiled faintly and hobbled to the door. "That lamp don't quite show enough, son." Slowly she opened the door, and as he took a step backward he heard its hinges squeaking even worse from inside.

But she gave him a reassuring smile, and without yet another visitor returned to her rocker. Then she rocked it more sideways to face him better. After this she began slowly rocking and speaking at about the same time. "How old you be, Hardrock?"

"I'm still nine. But in six weeks I'll be ten."

"You're sure a pretty child. Come here and let me see if you're real."

He looked from her toward the door and was relieved to see nothing to get excited about. Reassured of that he shrugged and advanced almost to her.

"But come closer where I can touch you."

After hesitating longer he did so and carefully she placed her hands on his sides. "You're still hot," she observed. "Running will do it." She pressed her hands down the sides of his pants to his bare knees. "Your legs so straight – your arms so strong – for a child. Yes, I think you know more than your age."

"Maybe so, widow." With this he took a definite step back and then nodded toward the doorway. "Hadn't you better shut it?"

But instead she answered, "Come here like before, son. An old woman needs more." When he declined she stared at him, then – of all things – carefully began nudging the bottom of her old-looking dress up her bony legs toward her knees.

He blinked, then in haste dug in his pocket and proudly brought out a five dollar bill. He spoke quickly, "Here's why mother sent me."

Though she kept her hands near her knees her dress stopped moving. "For – for me?" She seemed to decide it was, because suddenly she sat very still.

"Yes'm. Mother says prices at the commissary keep going up. Even bread."

"Even bread?"

"And when she didn't see you Saturday crossing the bridge to the store across the river, she said you could be broke, I think she said."

The widow stared.

"Mother wasn't certain, but she said, 'Let's be sure.'" Now he started toward her with the money.

However the widow, after a gasp, raised her hands from her knees and displayed her small palms toward him, defiantly. "I don't take help. What do you mean?"

He halted out of reach. "Mother heard your dead husband's pension maybe wasn't enough is all, Widow Turner. That was all she said and no more."

The widow abruptly sat as straight as the back of her rocker. "I don't know about you, son, but we don't take handouts here in these parts."

"But I don't think she meant it that way, widow."

"Life's too short for 'meants' to count." She ended in a tone almost as creaky as her door hinges moving slowly. Then she turned and nodded outside so hard her rocker moved a little. "You've every right to fear that great big creature. He eats things alive. He's guarding my road."

Hardrock stared. "What did you say?"

Abruptly she slapped her hands together, apparently for emphasis. "And has a big red tongue?"

"What?"

"I said a big red tongue?"

He thought about this carefully. "It looked to

me like he's got two of them."

Her laugh sounded like the door hinges were moving again. "Well he would. And a big wide face?"

Hardrock didn't have to think about this. "Oh yes. The biggest I ever saw. Like a log."

"Well you go tell your mama about it. And now scat while you can." She reached down abruptly, brought up the cane, and pointed it toward her doorway.

"You mean now?"

That strange laugh again. "Or walk if you want to, but I'd say run. He eats little boys running or walking." She angrily motioned her cane. "And take your money too. Your mama needs it more than me."

But he stared toward the door, still without moving.

She smiled at him. "You've got strong-looking arms and legs. You could outrun any snake I ever seen."

"If it's as big as this last one, I could sure try."

"I'll take that five dollar bill, after all. Bring it to me."

"I'll do that. Mother will be happy."

"Forget your ma. It makes me happy."

He returned to her, the bill dangling from his right hand. But instead of accepting the money she held his extended hand in both of hers. She laughed. "I can't take that bill just like that." She laughed again. "I can't take that bill just like that. Let me feel it."

He hesitated. "You don't want it?"

"First, put it on the mantel above the fireplace. Toward the middle of the fire where I can see it close."

"What? I mean you want me to hold this bill in front of your fireplace?"

"No, it's too hot. Put it near this end of the mantel. I can still see it."

"Well, sure." He strained to reach high enough, but his reach was about an inch too short.

"Here. I'll help you." She had risen from her rocker, and slipping a feeble arm around his waist she squeezed and helped him surmount that extra inch. Then she released him. Then he rearranged his clothes. The exercise had not been easy. "I'll tell mama you took it," he said.

"Tell her anything you like. I enjoyed helping you rise above yourself. What more can an old woman do?" She motioned the cane again. "Just as you wish. Except he gets hungrier by the minute from now till dark I hear."

He looked from the door to her, then again toward the door, and finally he sucked in his breath and steadily gained speed while exiting her cabin. He made it safely across the foot-log and down the road, and before reaching where he had seen his enemy he detoured enough to grab a stick about his own four and a half foot height, one that he figured wouldn't slow him much. His pounding heart made him feel like a coward, no matter what he did however.

He reached the place where he had seen his new acquaintance and soared across so fast he wasn't sure if he ever passed the right place or if he didn't. He was sure, though, that nothing would ever bring him up this Widow Turner hollow again.

His mother thanked him for "determination" with the widow, and then he hurried to his workout on the swinging bridge, one of his stepfather's major physical contributions to his life. Younger companions were rare on campuses such as Mountainside so his stepfather had shown him a solitary training exercise. In doing this, Hardrock stood alone near the middle of the swinging bridge and practiced tossing broken branches or pebbles from the proximity of his right ear to chosen targets on the Mighty Risky River.

2

THE MIGHTY RISKY
Anchors of Clay

Many strange things happened on the swinging bridge spanning the Mighty Risky River, but this may have been the strangest. Smeared in large letters on the side of an arriving truck were the words BROTHER ELFORD BOOST AND HIS DAUGHTER AMANDA. The bridge arched high, as if avoiding water, as well it should. As the bridge rumbled along its wires and cables and wood, Hardrock glanced again toward the Risky to see who was coming or going. He glimpsed a most beautiful sight—not the old man of course but the girl—in a flowing white cotton dress—almost flowing across the river.

Hardrock, now a teenager, who liked to dream, looked again out his school window and smiled. What if his mother sent him with a five-dollar bill to this young lady? On behalf of Mountainside he certainly welcomed her arrival.

He tried to think of the good, not the bad. Trouble seemed to follow the turbulent Mighty Risky River, so aptly named. A few years earlier, not far downstream from Free Fall, another preacher's daughter drowned at the Kentucky River dam. Bad things happened within Mighty Risky's banks and beyond its banks as well as high above.

Tall and lanky Brother Elford Boost, in a well-worn suit and shirt and tie, accompanied his 13-year-old daughter (the future Miss Appalachia), her hair in two braids and her calico dress stiffly starched. Across the Mighty Risky the Mountainside School bustled with school life. But one had to reach there first. Brother Boost cautioned his daughter, "Now, Amanda, dear, this swinging bridge can't do more than give you a good paddle." Her father laughed. "And who's going to paddle the prettiest little girl south of Alaska with her blonde hair in cute plaited braids and her big blue eyes smiling like a baby doll's?"

"I'm not really scared, Papa. I'm just suggesting that we go one at a time. Because both of us might shake the bridge too much." Amanda surveyed the unfriendly Mighty Risky too many truck lengths below. It looked rough and sounded rougher.

"Dear, you just don't weigh that much. Let's

face it. You're exactly right for your age, which is light. It wouldn't shake this bridge no more than a butterfly on a right-hand cable and the left-hand cable, or down below jumping from one bridge plank to the next."

She laughed. "All right. Then you start over, Papa. I'll follow." Again her quick laugh. "Unless you go over the side."

"If I do, the key's in the truck," he said just as jauntily. He started across, working his way along the steel hand-cable on each side, his feet creating a shaky rumble that eventually reached the opposite shore. Amanda followed, her progress causing a softer and gentler rumble across this river with its treacherous name.

Ashore on the campus end of the bridge they could have hailed a dozen or so students within hearing, but Brother Boost led their way staunchly to a nearby family-sized residence. "How do you know that's the building?" Amanda asked the confident-appearing preacher.

"Sweet, if you'd dreamed of your own parsonage as long as I have, you'd know one when you seen it. There. See that sign?"

"I do. MOUNTAINSIDE OFFICE ACROSS PORCH. Those directions seem a little unusual to me, Papa, but I guess they mean that we can go in across the porch and then knock on the office door and go on—supposing someone's in the office to let us in."

Brother Boost laughed. "Tell 'em, babe." They were confronted at the door by a powerful-looking man also wearing a shabby suit and coat and tie. After a good-natured chuckle the tall and slender visitor began, "Reverend Hope, I'd like to introduce my daughter, Amanda, sir. I'm Brother Elford Boost." He laughed. "Some might even call me Reverend, but the closest I came to graduating from seminary was Moody Bible Institute asking me to study Greek."

Hope smiled. "Come in and rest. I heard you crossing the bridge. You could already be tired."

"Well as a matter of fact, Reverend, we're late for our next star performance, one might say. I've been known to preach a little, I guess, and Amanda here invented music, you understand. So let's fish or cut bait—speaking of that bridge—and here goes." Brother Boost interrupted himself; however, to give Reverend Hope a hard stare as one might eye an animal prior to capture.

Hope seemed appropriately startled. "Cut bait, Brother Boost?"

Brother Boost let go slowly. "Indeed, sir. It seems that the great and sovereign state of Kentucky commonwealth claims I'm using child slave labor or something like that. They want this child to at least see a teacher while her eyesight lasts. So I'd like to bring her by twixt trips, sometimes, to work a little on her smarts, I guess you'd say."

Hope grinned. "She already looks smart enough to me. But yes—it's a great idea. Agree, Amanda?"

"I guess it depends a little doesn't it, Reverend Hope, if my smarts are only skin deep?"

Brother Boost's hand shot out to shake the Reverend's. "You're a man after my own heart, Reverend. And after my daughter too. We'll be in touch."

Hope shook his hand with enthusiasm. His eyes twinkled as the strange pair left him "to conquer the hills."

Hardrock's first introduction to Amanda came near the opening of the school's spring quarter and involved the worst flood in Mountainside history.

But dullness soon gave way to greater excitement. School had barely opened that Fall when the worst rain, remembered by anyone, fell in torrents. The rain without doubt qualified for the word "tide" used by some when emphasizing the word "flood." Reason for increased damage can be strip mining or simply timber cutting if practiced wantonly as at Burt Mines. Every acre deprived of foliage means one less warrior capturing valley-targeted rain water. Reverend Hope had not properly factored in land ravaging as he figured potential flood threats at Mountainside. Plus the fact that a man of God tends to anticipate bright sunlight, not dark clouds.

Then came the flood, worst ever at Mountainside. Of course anything to do with neighbor Burt Mines was worst, including destruction of forests. It was a fact unappreciated by Mountainside teachers and students as they lugged threatened items to safer sanctuary.

Hardrock was lugging a crowded bookcase from the library to the second floor of the parsonage. Not only lugging it but his chin was helping the bookcase door stay shut. In the upper room he found the president's wife, Mrs. Mary Hope, rearranging items. "Reverend Hope told me to bring this up here," he told her. "Where can I rest it?"

She smiled thanks. "On top of his desk, if you can lift that cabinet."

For answer Hardrock placed the cabinet on top.

"Thanks so very much," she said, "My husband, Reverend Hope, brought a computer a while ago."

"I know," Hardrock said, "He told me." Suddenly Hardrock stared toward the large glass window facing the Mighty Risky River. "There's that same truck," he said abruptly.

Indeed it was. Near the far end of the swinging bridge across the swollen river, with its large sign, probably about father and daughter, the truck was parked in water near the bumpers. A water pool had formed where the bank had been lowered to accommodate the end of the bridge. The truck apparently had been aimed past the end of the bridge, regardless of the flood overflowing the Risky River.

She went nearer the window. "That's Reverend Boost's truck, all right," she said. "He planned to bring her to school."

"Their truck drowned out," Hardrock said. "And their doors look jammed."

"Oh my," she said. "Aren't they in danger?"

"They at least need help. Excuse me," he said and bounded down the steps. "I'll see if I can make it," he called over his shoulder. He ran to the school's end of the swinging bridge and began advancing a few inches at a time. The planks here near this end were slippery but at least above water, unlike farther out nearer the middle of the bridge. There the flood was overpowering the bridge's planks as if angry at the intrusion.

His goal was to pull himself by the cable through the most dangerous waters. As he neared the middle of the bridge, he glanced toward the bridge's far end and saw that the truck's doors remained closed. His hands almost slipped on the cold railings, and he again concentrated on what he was doing. The submerged planks under his feet began to rumble violently and also slant more toward the bottom of the river.

Then suddenly he heard a loud noise. He gripped both railings. Ahead of him the truck began moving. It had dried enough to operate. He stared as it seemed to swim past the bridge.

Applause came from a crowd of observers on the campus. It was included in Hardrock's rise to fame.

During this "flood" or "tide" engulfing a valley that included the Mountainside parsonage, Reverend and Mrs. Hope found themselves knee-deep in the Mighty Risky water. "Water, water everywhere," Truman Hope remarked to his wife. "And unlike Noah, we don't have an ark."

She laughed with at least a part of her usual enthusiasm. "Including not a dove."

It was unrelenting. Mountainside was less than six miles from the river that bore the state's name. The mountains were so steep beside Kentucky's banks, rainwater became agitated.

"It's worse than anybody remembers," Hope added. "For what that's worth."

Faculty and students sloshed and waded across the campus, spreading word to clear all basements and then first floors as much as practical. "Rescue personal property and then school property as can be saved." The parsonage basement held many items, so the Hopes—assisted by roving bands of faculty and students—moved everything salvageable to the top floor. "At least it will be twice-blessed," Sister Mary pointed out.

"You okay, Reverend? Mrs. Hope?" It was math instructor Frank Hammer wading more than knee deep onto the parsonage back porch. His clothes looked wet to his waist. "Is it as deep in there as out here? Looks like it."

"Are you all right?" Reverend Hope asked. "Or should I ask? As for this house, I really don't think it'll budge." Hope spoke proudly. He had been one of a dozen or so volunteers to build the parsonage. "So far it hasn't even shuddered."

The Mighty Risky, no longer simply a river but now a lake north of the Kentucky, at least seemed less boisterous than usual. "Truman says if it climbs another half foot inside the parsonage we'll abandon ship," Mary said. "I guess that's the phrase. And then rush out and help others salvage what they can."

"It doesn't look much worse than an hour ago," Truman repeated. "It hasn't risen much in the last couple hours though it hasn't gone down either. And this latest drizzle isn't getting worse, at least."

"Praise the Lord," Hammer said.

Truman nodded. "We certainly won't expect the worst. I'll look around here for a couple minutes before heading out again around the campus. Mary can stay here checking around for anything else to go upstairs."

"I'll wait and go with you," Hammer said.

"Good."

Later that evening Reverend Hope returned to the parsonage upstairs, and exhausted, he and his wife tried to get some sleep lying on the floor wrapped in blankets. The Reverend planned to come down every hour to check on the water level.

It is probable that neither of the Hopes slept much that night, perhaps Mary in particular. If everyone has their own special fear, as it's said, then hers was fear of drowning. It may have been that she slipped in a tub as a child, or simply slid into a puddle of water wearing her Sunday best. But the idea of anything associated with rivers or boats had been one of her major problems. That is why what happened that night had a lasting effect. Shortly before midnight Reverend Hope checked the flood level in the house and was more convinced than ever that the flood had crested. The water was 24 to 26 inches deep on the first floor, surely the crest. Thirty minutes later he checked again. He was convinced that the Mighty Risky had indeed crested and that probably, as early as the following morning, it might start going down. There were no more sheets of cascading waterfalls down precipitous mountainsides to keep the Kentucky flooded. So the Hopes went to bed, Reverend Hope planning to wait an hour before going down for another safety check.

The Hopes were no more than warm under the covers when there was a loud "hello" from the dark wetness outside. Truman made his way sleepily to a window. Somewhere out there was the amazing, startling sight of a rowboat-sized vessel manned by two boatmen with a lantern in the middle riding over the parsonage yard fence. "Is anyone home?" one of them called, rowing onto the porch, paddling and grabbing portions of the building.

They said they had come because a woman in the valley was in labor and was surely going to have her baby this night. They wondered if Mrs. Hope could come help.

Sister Hope herself called down with the answer. "Wait just a moment, I'm coming." So she dressed, filled her large purse with the things she would need, put on a hat, and started valiantly down the stairs. As she did so her husband and a husky student from the school waded through the water at the bottom part of the stairway to help her into the boat.

The water seemed twice as cold as it was because the Hopes had just gotten out of bed. Reverend Hope and his helper made an "arm-carry," and Mary Hope climbed down to just above water level and sat on their arms, balancing her own around their shoulders. They waded out of the house, Mary holding her feet above the water. She felt that if she could get to the boat she could make it the rest of the way, so she prayed that the Lord would "especially strengthen those who were carrying her, and that her husband and the student would not trip over anything in the water." At the boat the waiting boatmen helped her up into it, and then paddled their vessel with their new passenger in it into and out of the doorway.

It seemed possible that no one ever again would see the passengers, or even the boat. It reminded Reverend Hope of a dream, possibly a nightmare, as it began disappearing right over the yard fence between the silver maple trees, then turned upstream across the campus and out behind the girl's dormitory with the two men paddling away. The lantern on the boat made very necessary light as they continued toward the waiting mother-to-be.

Sister Hope arrived in time to help, and things went well. "A very fine baby girl was born that night" as Sister Mary Hope continued a practice that resulted in, among other things, so many girls in the area with a first name of Mary. While Sister Hope delivered babies, Reverend Hope was trying to keep them alive at a time of neighborhood violence – and the Burt mines never ending desire to take over the school property for its hidden black treasure.

Reverend Hope entitled one of his early sermons "Bullets by the Numbers" and for good cause. One morning about daybreak a welcoming committee arrived outside the parsonage. Truman and Mary were not yet up when they heard a loud "hello" from the front gate. "Mr. Hope, we want to see you." Truman got up, put on his slippers, with a raincoat over his nightgown, and then hurried out onto the porch. Just outside the yard two horsemen featured pistols and holsters at their sides. One stationed himself slightly in front of the other, his weapon more than the others, seeming to reflect the cold morning Appalachian sky.

In response to this possibly ominous intrusion Truman gripped a porch post as if to squeeze out potential problems. But he was surprised at the evenness of his tone as in his usual deep baritone voice he spoke loudly. "Good morning, friends. What can I do to help you today?"

They did not reply at once but finally the one in front said, "We were going through and stopped to see how you are."

"We are fine, thank you. We hope you're fine. Is there anything I can do for you?"

"No, we'll just be going on," the speaker replied. "We just stopped to see you."

Truman went back to tell Mary what had happened. He stated that it seemed a little odd that visitors would get them out of bed barely after daybreak to ask about his health, but if that's the way around here, he was glad things came out as they did. Mary got up and fixed breakfast and they went about the day's work.

A few days later Truman was at the Free Fall post office. As he left, a man took him aside and said in a low voice, "Reverend Hope, did two men come down to your house on horseback the other morning and ask to see you early in the day?"

"Yes, they did," Truman agreed. "I thought it was a little unusual."

"I'll tell you, Reverend Hope, what they came for. Seventeen miners who work in county mines had a meeting. They decided that the school is on coal they want and also that you're causing too much trouble for the moonshiners. So somebody without a grudge ought to be the one to get you killed. So they selected two men who agreed to come down to your house and shoot you."

Truman said, his eyes a little wider, "They came, talked just briefly, then left. I wondered about it at the time. After what you tell me I still wonder."

The other said, "I can tell you the word that's going around as to why they didn't shoot you. They drew straws for the one to do it, but after they'd ridden away he told the one with him, 'I simply can't shoot down a man who starts right off the first thing in the morning by calling me a friend and then asks what he can do to help.' So what you said turned him away from his plan."

Truman went home and decided to share this with Mary. He felt it would be more reassuring than frightening. Their religion had given them a peaceful response to crisis at the school. As he said in a sermon, "They had learned that they couldn't feel more frightened because they felt they were beyond being scared."

Then one day Lotus Livingston—a strapping and large teenager—arrived on campus. Standing courteously straight in Truman Hope's office he explained his mission. "Mr. Hope, I'm asking to enroll in your school. But first I've got to come clean."

Hope's stocky frame stiffened slightly.

"I wouldn't feel right about joining up at Mountainside without clearing some air."

"Well, we're certainly glad that you're interested in our school. What's troubling about attending here?"

Lotus blushed. "I know I've got to tell you this. It just hurts, is all."

"Lotus, you may remember that the Bible says, 'Come let us reason together.' So what's the problem, young man, that we need to talk out?"

Lotus dug into the hip pocket of his overalls and retrieved a bullet that for whatever reason looked unusually large and shiny, a projectile Lotus now extended. "My pa was the one what came by to kill you that morning the seventeen drew lots. But whoever won, they gave the bullet to my pa and told him to bring back your head."

Truman blanched slightly. "I assume that's just a figure of speech. I think he mainly meant to shoot me."

"Yes. Right through the heart."

Truman continued somewhat hurriedly. "Why did they give the bullet to your pa—or why did they name him to do the killing?"

Lotus straightened even more. "That one's easy," he said simply. "Pa's known as the best shot in Kentucky." He sounded proud. "He can shoot the eye out of a gnat so clean it'd look like he's got glass eyes."

Lotus still extended the bullet, so Truman took it. "I'll certainly be pleased to keep it. And accept it as a token of forgiveness, if that's what you want." Then partly to change the subject Truman said, "Let me show you another one." From his desk drawer he brought a bullet flattened at its end. "This one was actually fired my way. So, Lotus, how could I nurture a grudge about one not even fired."

Lotus stared, "That one was fired your way?"

"Yes it was. It was fired from outside our chapel window and shattered the wires holding the light over my pulpit while I was preaching. That marksman must have practiced on a few gnats himself."

Lotus checked a grin. "Oh yeah, I heard about that. And you went right on preaching in the dark."

"Well not exactly in the dark," Hope said wryly. "I had help."

Lotus's face sobered. "I know. I'm already a believer too, Mr. Hope. I sure would appreciate gettin' into your school. No matter what my pa once done."

"Well a couple of bullets certainly won't stop us. Absolutely not. Let me show you around the school, Lotus, and find out what kind of studies you have in mind."

3

BILLY BOB
Face Lift

At Mountainside School, alongside snake-handling minister the Reverend Henry Boost strolled a recent graduate from Eddyville prison, the Reverend Billy Bob Berry. Or that is recently released from Eddyville on good behavior after serving faithfully for twelve years.

"Makes you wish you were back in school, eh, Billy Bob?" the Reverend Boost asked.

"In spades. Hell—yes. In spades."

"Billy Bob, where we're walking now was almost a cemetery very recently. Last month a couple of pilots decided they wanted to be the first to land a plane near Free Fall. So they called in and asked Truman Hope, who runs this place, if he saw any problems."

"Problems?"

"Well, as you can see by looking around, Reverend Billy Bob, landing in this place is like landing on an iceberg, without the cold. As you can see, the mountains come together at the end of the valley, and once you fly in here the only way out is down."

"Yeah."

"So those pilots wanted to know how flat the campus is."

"It sure as hell looks flat to me."

"Reverend Billy Bob. The language. It is flat. As Brother Hope told them, 'As flat as a mother's hand.'"

"In spades."

"I guess that means correct. Anyway, here they come breezing in from the south, the only way they could get in—as happy as a couple of ducks at a waterfall—as their wheels touch down before a lot of people waiting to see them land. Billy Bob, do you see that school barn a couple hundred yards down the valley facing the campus?"

"Sure. Go ahead."

"Well, it's a barn without doors. Brother Hope had neglected to tell the pilots about a fence running east and west about halfway down the campus. So in trying to avoid the fence they did what they call a ground loop, and when it was all over they were sitting inside that barn without any wings on their plane or doors on the barn. They say the first thing you do if you have a wreck is turn the engine off so your plane doesn't explode. Remembering this, the pilot yelled to his co-pilot,

"Turn off that engine."

The co-pilot said, "That's not the engine you're listening to. That's my knees."

Billy Bob asked, "Is the plane still in there?"

"No. They hauled it out in coal trucks once the Union said okay. I don't know why I told you that," Brother Boost added. "It's got nothing to do with the real problem on the table."

"That word 'table' reminds me. I'm starting to get hungry."

"As my official guest, the dining hall will serve you along with other adults. I do appreciate your offering to help me in my revival campaign, Brother Billy Bob. I can't think of a better way to raise crowds. Maybe even up the collection ante a little bit. The Reverend Bill Bob Berry. Saved at Eddyville. Released on good behavior after only twelve years."

"Spare me the details," Billy Bob blurted.

"My real problem is my stepson Hardrock," Brother Boost declared. "I'm afraid my wife is trying to make him into some kind of queer."

"Holy—what I mean is, what did you say?"

"Ever since I insisted on naming him Hardrock she's been trying to prove that he's non-violent or something like that. She forevermore keeps coming back to that Bible verse that says turn the other cheek. She's had him wearing short pants until he entered high school. Until he was almost old enough to wear a cane. What I mean is, Billy

Bob, my dad was also a preacher and I got knocked around quite a bit, and I don't intend for Hardrock to be a 'Nellie bar the door' too late either."

"That I can hear," Billy Bob agreed.

"So every time I have a chance I ease him over to the locker room at the gym, close the door, and we start going at each other like a couple of violents, and I don't mean violets."

"There you go, Henry. You and I see eye-to-eye."

"I must admit my deciding to invite you for the revival campaign was because I kept thinking good publicity. Such as, 'Come and hear Reverend Billy Bob Berry, champion heavyweight boxer for the entire prison. Saved by grace. A born-again Christian.'"

"You want me to be a good example for your son Hardrock? Show him how?"

"Right on the button. Give him a few light taps. Show him how a real boxer does it. Like you said."

"Let the other guy grab you first, or the police will grab you by the collar. Knock his arm just a little off center. Just enough to miss you. Then come in with all you got. My not doing exactly that got me retirement at Eddyville. I came in first, the other guy went down first, and the gates crashed on me."

"Now is as good a time as any," Brother Boost

declared. "Most everybody is heading for the dining hall."

"It'd d—we better have."

A helpful student intercepted Hardrock for them, and the youth joined his father and the fellow minister at the gym. Introductions were brief. "Hardrock, this is the preacher I've been telling you about," Brother Boost greeted his stepson. "We've got to leave for a revival this evening, but first I wanted you to see how it's done by a pro. First, let me show him how you and I always do a little sparring." From a nearby locker Brother Boost claimed two pairs of boxing gloves and gaily tossed one pair to his son.

The boxing proved to be a good show. Both of them dodging, and then coming in with light blows.

"See what I mean, Billy Bob, how he hangs in? From a 'pro' viewpoint, would you practice any different?"

"They call 'em love pats', Henry. For a practice to really count, you've got to hear some heads snap. When I won the Eddyville national championship, they claimed they could hear me all the way to Solitaire, Kentucky."

Brother Boost studied his son. "You up to trying a few, Hardrock?"

Hardrock slipped on the gloves without enthusiasm. "Well if I have to," he mumbled. He and Billy Bob exchanged a couple of light jabs. Billy

Bob proved correct. You let the other jab first, shoving it aside at the last moment.

Hardrock came on with a single blow after his jab.

Billy Bob, like that unfortunate airplane, landed too hard, in his case flat on his back, his arms and legs outstretched. They might have heard the blow in Solitary, but Billy Bob didn't.

Hardrock reached down for him immediately. "Oh, I'm really sorry, Reverend. I really am. Dad and I always follow through with the jab. I really am sorry, Reverend. Dad, can you help with his other arm?"

"Son," Brother Boost said. "You'd better hurry for your vittles at our dining hall. At one point Billy Bob said he was hungry."

"Sure, Dad. But please do convince Reverend Berry that I really didn't mean to."

"I said they're about to start serving, son. Do I have to put it in writing?"

4

DOLLY SIMMONS
The Last Meeting

Every time Hardrock tried to do someone a good turn, it cost him. When he was nine Widow Turner rejected his five. Then his high school days featured Dolly Simmons. She had ridden an 18-wheeler into the motel's parking lot east of Free Fall, and when the truck left, Dolly had not. Instead she married the motel's owner, Charlie Grundy, resulting in a bumpy marriage that lasted only three months, after which Grundy's divorce papers left her the motel if she would leave him alone. And now, in rooms 6 and 10, it looked like every Arab in the country was coming in.

Of course this assumed that Abbas and Samir, or so identified on the phone, would actually arrive in rooms 6 and 10. Not only that, the "camel pushers" were reserving their rooms for both Friday and Saturday.

Certainly the River Motel in the past had always been "more local." In fact, some nights there had been no one to help her survive her solitude. Actually, on some occasions there had been no activity at all except the Risky River on the western side of the river road.

The only thing missing in this room-rental business of course was a knight in white shining armor. She had fully believed that once she dumped Grundy, such a knight would come barreling along in weeks if not days. But so far only one-night stands had resulted, or at the most three-night. That's one reason Hardrock Adams caught her eye. He'd looked different, so much more clean cut than the average student. Yes, she needed some real loving, and Hardrock Adams seemed like the kind of boy she could learn to love in a short time. He was on the swinging bridge, headed straight toward her if she hurried—and she flat out meant to. She greeted him before he stepped from the bridge. "What a pleasant surprise. I didn't know that bigwigs from the school ever got this far off the beaten path."

"Well, they do, or at least I am." They halted to face each other at the end of the bridge. "As a matter of fact," he added, "I was headed for the motel. Reverend Hope asked me to make sure that the two Middle Eastern visitors feel like this is their home away from home and otherwise get directions."

She laughed. "You can count on it." She meant in particular that Hardrock could count on her. She would always insist that he was not too young for her thirty years, though she might be too old for his eighteen or thereabouts. "When I find out exactly how many Arabs there are, I'll know how to fix their rooms. I could sure use some hurried-up help to make some beds."

"If I see someone who looks like a bed-maker, I'll direct them straight to you. As for the Outreach Program, Reverend Hope is planning a first class visit. He's been working on this program for some time now. A Christian Outreach Program. They've already started two groups near Baghdad."

"Well I'm sure glad to learn it. It's crazy. They came in one car and rent two rooms, 6 and 10, about as far apart as I offer. And dressed. They're either wearing nightgowns or robes, I tried to tell which."

Suddenly a car eased into the motel parking lot, drove as far as Number 6, then made a U-turn and headed back out and north toward nearby Quicksand.

"Again, they're from the Middle East," he said. "They're different. Well, I'd better get to running before Reverend Hope starts looking for me again. Good luck."

"I'll need it," Dolly affirmed.

"Bye," Hardrock said and began running south alongside the paved river road. Reverend Hope had used his influence as head of Mountainside to have the road paved well, and Hardrock ran swiftly. Also, he could feel her scrutiny though already separated the length of a football field. Then she returned to the motel, reluctantly. She ended at the utility room next to her office, and then with several towels and wash cloths as alibis she continued along the sidewalk toward their rooms. Her dress felt a little tight, and she remembered how men in general stared at it. That thought made her wonder about men in general and she sighed. She wished she sounded as confident as the Risky.

She stopped at Room 10 and after a few seconds of listening knocked. Grundy had maintained that the only real profit in running a rundown something like the River Motel was what you learned about people. As he'd said in one of his more sober moments, you could learn more about a person glancing at their room than you could listening to a thousand lies.

She knocked louder. "Room service," she called in gaily. Well, so be it. Cradling the towels and wash cloths in her left arm, she fished the pass key from her dress pocket and entered the room.

But then, of all things, she found herself staring at his photograph on the dresser. Horror of horrors, it showed him standing apparently beside a wife and two teenage children. Not only that, a good-looking man and wife too, to say nothing of the children. Indeed, a happily married family man who takes his family picture with him traveling! She sighed and then, her shoulders sagging, backed from the room and closed the door.

It was lucky that she'd done so, too, because at this moment she saw parked in front of her office the car that a few minutes earlier had cruised her parking lot. Except that now a tall dark-complexioned man emerged from the car and after an impatient look toward the locked office stood staring toward her.

She laughed quickly. "Just a minute," she called. "Hold your horses please."

The man had left his car engine running as if to emphasize willingness to throw his weight around. Still, approaching him she couldn't help but notice that he looked strangely like the Arab who checked into 10, except his clothes. Say 39 or 40, tall and muscular, and in some ways almost as good looking as that Hardrock Adams.

"I had to take some towels to a room." She smiled as she unlocked her office door and entered, and then he smiled as he turned to enter also. "How can I help you?" she said from behind the counter.

He glanced, no longer smiling, toward her registration ledger. "Abbas and Samir."

"Oh," she answered brightly. "I knew it was you, though. It's a pleasure having you, Mr. Abbas Al Kahil if that's you and not him." Her smile emphasized genuine pleasure indeed. Hardrock Adams was more appealing in a boyish kind of way, but Mr. Abbas Al Kahil, maybe the right name, looked more rugged, which was good, though she hoped that didn't mean "meaner" as well. Charlie Grundy had also looked rugged. She lifted the registration sheet slightly and did so without lowering her smile. Perhaps she should have looked down, however. Her excited hands almost pushed the form off the counter.

"My partner gave the wrong information," he said. "Here. I'll check it." Before she could object he scanned the register and returned it to her without even a "Thank you."

Her customer's hands ended palms up on the counter, reminding her that his hands were too smooth for a coal miner and for that matter any hard labor.

"I'm really not supposed to let you read other people's records." At least Grundy had told her about that. For response her customer lifted both hands slightly off the counter, stared at her a moment, then hurried out to his car and drove to his room. But then suddenly she found herself staring even harder toward the place across the counter he'd just vacated. Before really realizing it she went to the front window and turned the sign to read NO VACANCY. Next she took a glass from under her office counter and hurried with it to her bedroom where she rescued a bottle of bourbon from that same dresser drawer and loaded the bottom third of her glass. As she drank she began glancing more and more first at her telephone and then the office door and then the bottle of "kickapoo juice" waiting on her dresser. After perhaps a half dozen gulps she emptied her glass, then picked up her phone and dialed the number 10.

He lifted his receiver on the first ring, which might or might not be a good sign. "Mr. Abbas Al Kahil, if this is you, this is the front desk. I'm sitting up here in my bedroom all alone having a drink, and more and more I keep worrying about a puzzle." She laughed. "I just keep thinking that maybe ten years ago I knew someone who looked really an awful lot like you. And I do mean an awful lot."

He said nothing.

"Are you able to hear me, Mr. Abbas Al Kahil?"

"Uh huh."

"Well it's simple, John—can I call you John?"

This time silence again.

"Anyway, John, that big hulk of a man I knew then was—well how can we say it—I guess the word is 'close.' I was young enough to be his daughter, he said." She laughed. "Come to think about it you and I are young enough to be his son and daughter now. Maybe I've had too much to drink. But Dale could drink—great man alive—you talk about drink."

"I'm not talking about anything. You're the one talking."

"Oh now, John. John, I didn't mean to make you mad. I'm sorry. I'll hang up."

He replaced his phone quite a bit sooner than she found herself able to. Then she retrieved the bottle off the dresser and attempted to pour herself a drink approximately the same size as before. But it was nearer a half than a third. She tried to focus toward her wristwatch, but the ringing of her telephone eventually caught her attention. After more than one unsuccessful try she lifted the receiver. "Dolly Simmons speaking. And yes we do have no bananas. Or make that no motel rooms—you have, but I don't."

It was John, or make that Burt. She was ninety-nine percent sure. "If you please. I got your puzzle. Who am I?"

"Oh—who are you?" She giggled. "Starting where?"

"Try me."

She giggled louder. "I'd like to, Burt—oh how I would. In memory of your dad, let's say."

"My dad likes parties, doesn't he?"

She hesitated, trying to think more clearly. "I could ease down there for just a little warm-up party, if you really mean it, Burt. As they say, two's a party and three's a crowd."

"No. Give me time for a quick shave. Then I'll be up there at your place."

He replaced his receiver with a bang before she could cradle hers. But the more she thought about it the more she realized that her place shouldn't be it for either a warm-up or a party itself. Not till after midnight, at least. And though she maybe looked like a Cinderella—Grundy certainly said she did on a number of occasions—she was not one to wait for midnight with or without a pair of shoes.

The clock read somewhere between eight and nine—still plenty of time—and she wrapped her bourbon bottle in the towels and wash cloths, locked her office door with an unbelievable amount of hits and misses, and then began making her way as carefully as she could along the sidewalk to Room 10.

Now was a good time to think of that thing about, "If Mohammed won't come to the mountain, the mountain will come to Mohammed." Could they possibly have meant the River Motel? If so, this one must be Mohammed. Then she must certainly be the mountain. Well no one could remove her.

She almost walked straight into the woods past 10—well, not exactly straight—she giggled and tried a step backward. Slowly she made her left arm claim her bundle. She was good at this, but ordinarily she didn't go around carrying bourbon along with it either. She giggled and lifted her right arm. The bottle didn't slide free—what a near catastrophe! She knocked, or didn't she? She tried it again. She believed he heard it this time.

There was a long silence. Then Burt said, "Okay," or was it "Jose?" Whatever, he at least opened the door.

She almost lost her balance as she followed the opening door in. As she struggled to regain her balance she found herself in his arms, her left arm continuing to hold her bundle though not really knowing why.

"Beautiful." He pressed his lips against hers, and his hands moved up her back to her neck. Her neck snapped quickly but her body took several seconds to reach the floor, and though not a large woman she bounced loudly on impact. He caught the bundle in time to keep it from crashing with her.

Suddenly guttural sounds started escaping her throat as she gasped for air, and her arms and legs began flailing spasmodically. He stepped at once to the door, closed it, and returned to kneel beside her. For some reason her tight dress made her resemble a slaughtered calf, or perhaps cow, wrapped in cellophane, her breasts on one side and her rear on the other. He jerked a towel free and slammed it against her throat. There would be no evidence of hand prints through this cloth. Then he grabbed the towel on both sides of her throat and began the deadly process of resting his 220 pounds on it. This had the double advantage of strangling her and at the same time stifling a faint scream that she seemed to be trying to make. Instead her arms and legs flailed more wildly now as might a professional wrestler's pinned to a mat, her tight dress nonetheless working its way toward her waist so that she too appeared to be wearing tights. She tried another scream but now he jerked the towel around her neck, and her attempted screams began subsiding. Bright blood started flowing from her mouth and nose. Her last breaths smelled to him like a strange concoction of alcohol and death. Finally the blue coloring in her face ended as her body went limp. He tried not to look at her face as it died.

He rose slowly, in his excitement almost losing his balance. His stomach suddenly felt like it was bloated by moonshine distilled by using the old formula "make it to sell but not to drink." He had never before killed a woman who had simply come to his room to make love. Also, maybe adding to her bad luck was marijuana, the mountain's best cash crop. But, anyway, this little lady had experienced a pleasant death compared to what people like Abbas Al Kahil would do to you if he thinks you're an alcoholic. Too bad, but this time it had to be her.

He jerked a sheet off his bed and rolled her roughly in it as indeed one might a carcass. Then he eased open his door and looked outside. No one in sight, an absence that thankfully included not even a Kentucky hillbilly. So he walked to his car trunk and opened it. Then he hurriedly returned inside, picked up the body as one might a sleeping child—she was not that heavy—then carried her out and rolled her into the car trunk, slamming the door quickly. Again inside his room, his door once more locked, he began tidying up, first by soaking a towel with cold water and as carefully wiping all visible signs of blood from the carpet.

Suddenly there was a knock on the door. After a final look around the room he called out, "Abbas Al Kahil."

"Room service," Abbas Al Kahil's voice answered after a faint laugh.

It was the first real encounter with death in Hardrock's young life.

5

RIPPING PAPER IN SHREDS
Torn Together

His stepfather's snake-handling reputation followed Hardrock. One reason was Buck Burt, son of the area's top mine owner, Rodney Burt. The rich man's reason for sending his son to Mountainside instead of some costly eastern school was not known. Was he so tight he wanted to save a few dollars tuition? Was he so determined to mine the school for coal he wanted a traitor in the Mountainside camp? Whatever the reason, the son, Buck Burt, thoroughly disliked Hardrock. But "why" was harder to explain. Their background, perhaps. Buck's father was a great financial leader in the area, and Hardrock's stepfather swapped coal-mining for snake-handling.

One of Buck's shows of dislike occurred in a Mountainside classroom. For starters, emphasizing their differences, they sat apart. Their teacher was late, and Buck used the occasion to snatch a sheet of paper out of a classmate's hands and scribble on it the words SNAKE ADAMS and then start the paper along the students near him.

The note elicited laughter from each recipient except Hardrock, who glimpsed the derisive words, and Amanda Boost, who exuded charm from behind Buck. Instead of laughing she accepted the paper by ripping it into shreds and letting them fall on Buck, from behind. Buck was exceedingly angry and drew back a fist, but what male south of the Mason Dixon line would strike a beautiful girl classmate?

"Let me have another sheet," Burt demanded of his first pal but only to be thwarted as the teacher arrived.

After class was over, Hardrock showed his gratitude to the girl. "Let me help you with some of those books."

"That does help."

As they left the classroom he said, "Thank you for tearing up that note. It saved me the trouble."

"My father sees me leaving the class and is here to take me home."

"I'll bet he's that determined-looking man headed this way now." Hardrock shifted several of her textbooks from his right hand to his left. "I'll be pleased to meet him."

"Well, you're about to. He must be running late."

"Hi, sweet," her father called past a number of students. "Here I am."

Then he apparently saw the lack of books in his daughter's hands and the overflow in Hardrock's. "You don't need help carrying your books, child."

"That's all right, Papa. He was kind enough to help me. You've seen Hardrock before."

"Hi, Hardrock. Honey, if you'd claimed these books are heavy, I could meet you at the building. Certainly you're not that weak, are you? You could leave the books behind if you want to, and I could get them all myself and we could take it from there." He eagerly accepted Hardrock's offer of an armful. "Certainly she doesn't need help carrying her books."

"I certainly won't carry them if you're around" Hardrock said. "Thanks for your help."

Brother Boost stared. "You helped her?"

"But she helped me first."

"Let's go, sweet."

Her father embraced her books and then pulled his daughter to him.

"Thanks." At that she seemed a little reluctant, as she left.

6

THE OUTSIDER
A Ten Foot Pole

Hardrock had done several goofy things in his life, but this turned out to be the goofiest. He had observed Amanda and her father come across the bridge, and asked if there were any chores he could do that might help.

Yes, as a matter of fact there was. They were visiting the campus this Friday afternoon because of the sickness of Brother Henry Boost, Hardrock's stepfather and Elford's brother. It seems that Brother Henry's close friend in West Virginia had been bitten by a five-foot rattlesnake and had died this morning at daybreak.

Brother Henry did not feel like attending a snake-handling service scheduled this evening, so Brother Elford Boost had agreed to fill in, without snakes. Elford accepted Hardrock's offer to drive

and soon they were riding on the river road between the vertical mountainside and the river.

Brother Boost reflected on the seriousness of
the situation. "Elder Otha Slocum, who was killed
by the rattler last night in Tennessee, well he and
my brother Henry are—make that were—were
best of friends, and that same snake almost bit
him once before. That's why we're substituting for
Henry tonight."

"What a terrible thing," Amanda said.

"That's one reason, child, I wouldn't touch one
of them with a ten-foot pole, including Brother
Henry's favorite rattler Jezebel now resting comfortably in her cage inside our truck."

"Where is this Pentecostal Church we're supposed to be going to?" she asked.

In an obvious attempt to lighten the conversation, Brother Boost said "A fer piece as they say.
Trinity Church Pentecostal."

"Where is Trinity Pentecostal again, Papa?"

"Well, Trinity Church Pentecostal ain't all that
close. So we had better hit the breeze in time to
make that big four-stater tonight, Nelly."

"Where is Trinity Pentecostal again, Papa?
You'll remember I've never been there."

"The reason you ain't is because it seems to
cater more to high falutin' Sunday folks than to
Evangelist crowds. It's one of the best churches
in this part of Eastern Kentucky, in my opinion.

Electricity, indoor plumbing, wood painted white instead of white cement blocks. Elder Otha Slocum preached there some times, and he was a go-getter from the word go, if I may say so."

"Was he in charge of the convention?" Hardrock asked absently. "I never have got that clear."

Elford chuckled. "No, and I guess that's where you come in, Hardrock, my boy."

"Papa, why don't you go ahead and tell him the whole thing?" She smiled gently toward Hardrock. "Snake-handling believers don't have a national organization, so when they hold a conference it's even more important. Elder Slocum calls Papa 'the Dean of Evangelists in Southeastern Kentucky' and so he made him Vice President."

"Now, now," Elford objected modestly. "It's not that big a deal is it, dear? Top handlers from Kentucky, Tennessee, Georgia, and West Virginia are coming, that's true. Frankly, of course, they'll bring their best and biggest snakes too."

Hardrock's face warmed slightly. "I'm certainly not trying to be flippant, Reverend Boost, but why the best and biggest? Jesus doesn't say, 'And they shall pick up the best and biggest serpents' does He? He just says 'and they shall pick up serpents', and also of course speak in unknown tongues."

Reverend Boost chuckled slightly. "That's a good question, but I think the answer is our church—as my brother Henry sees it—don't want people calling what we're doing a cop-out, as they might if we used a little three-inch scorpion for instance. We're supposed to be proving the power of God so that others can go and do likewise, certainly. I reckon, too, as long as you're jumping hurdles, you might as well pick something big, God or no God."

"That is a good question, Hardrock," Amanda said. "I've wondered about that too. But, as Papa's heard, some of the preachers as well as laymen seem almost to spoil their snakes. They often swap with each other to get ones they like better after meetings are over."

"Amen," Brother Elford said.

"Again, as Papa's heard, after a large handling service it sometimes looks like a country fair or maybe a good old-fashioned cattle auction. I'll swap this big timber rattler or diamond back for that cottonmouth or beautiful copperhead, things like that. Trying to help each other—not for profit though, of course."

"I could never do that," Hardrock said.

"It's really no big deal, son, or even a bad one either," Brother Elford said. "They have to be found some way. If they can't be found in some nearby woods, there are usually people around a handling, selling 'em. For far too much, of course. For sometimes as much as a hundred dollars, I keep hearing."

"I find that hard to accept."

"Oh sure, Hardrock. Many handlers grow fond of their serpents and even give them pet names as they say, like Rainbow, because of their pretty colors, or plain old names like Pretty Boy or Jezebel, or such. Snakes can live a couple dozen years or more in the wild, but many last only a year or so being handled—so of course they've got to be replaced."

"Papa, where is that Born Again Episcopal Church? Again, how do we get there?"

"Of course we don't concentrate all that much on just snake handling, Hardrock. You've seen the Mason jars of strychnine some folks lug around. All them, others too. Such as blow torches, if anybody feels the calling to overpower heat. Of course, healing is still a big thing too, though I don't expect healing to be featured in tonight's four-stater." He turned toward his daughter. "You say what, Amanda?"

"Neither of us has ever seen that Born Again church, Papa. Where is it?"

"Well for starters, it's between Hazard and Harlan, say a hundred miles north and south and about that many miles expanding east and west— that big an area." Elford laughed. "Of course I'm not trying to confuse you. But in my humble opinion that's some of the roughest hundred square miles east of the Mississippi—again as others say, not just me." He looked toward Hardrock. "You know where Slocum Branch is, don't you, Hardrock? Kentucky Highway 81 maybe?"

"Well on 81 exactly twenty miles south of Stuttsville, without much else surviving there, between there and Harlan proper, there's an old sawmill on one side and across the highway an even bigger one and older. Just past them two sawmills you've got a sign and an arrow pointing to the right to 'Born Again' along a gravel road up a winding hollow. After about three miles it dead-ends at the church. You can't miss it."

Amanda exclaimed, "Why—about twenty miles—the church sign—on down south of Stuttsville—points right—just says church."

"Which is what I'd call 'Scratch Off Acres'," Elford added. "Don't even slow down for missing bridges over the Mighty Risky—which you mighty well better—or flashing stop signs or deer in the road if I may. In other words, Stuttsville isn't the place a true law-abiding Christian wants to get caught. I don't plan to get caught in Stuttsville again until the good guys really take charge of what's there."

"I can think of some good things" Amanda said.

"Well, I've got the answer. Hardrock sits on the back bench. He doesn't handle snakes, but he does handle the boys. As I said."

"Papa," Amanda said.

Elford laughed. "They see Hardrock back there it's all Nellie wrote. They'll take off like Sherman through Georgia."

"What's this all about?" Hardrock said.

"Papa, why do you leave people dangling like that? Tell him what is what."

"I don't mind, Hardrock." Elford said. "Hardrock, as I said, some of the tough boys on the mountainside enjoy poking fun at snake handlers. They sit on the back bench and ease out the door ever so often, not only for a smoke or a drink or dope or a loud laugh and sometimes they call back inside."

"And I'm supposed to keep them under control?" Hardrock said.

"That's one way to put it," Elford agreed.

"Uncle Henry sometimes sits back there," Amanda added. "But, as you heard, he has a headache."

"Speaking of who is where. I definitely plan to ask my good friends, the approximate half dozen snake handlers, to keep the snakes in their hands or on their bodies but not on the platform, if I may. That's reserved for Amanda and me. Let's be clear, I'm definitely not making fun of the handlers. They're dedicated Christians—often leaders of the community—things like that."

As they bounced toward the church, a worshipper bore a large cage through the church front doorway. Elford glanced aside to Jezebel and said "Stay tight." Then as they arrived he said, "I'll bring Jezebel in as needed."

Reverend Elford Boost made it in time, all right. That is he preceded his two companions into the sanctuary and made it along the right side to the platform and then to the pulpit. "Good evening, folks," he greeted almost fifty worshipers already convened. "I'm sorry to be running late, as they say, but I bring you a message of great importance. Elder Hiram Slocum, who a few of you may have met, was bit by a rattler last night in his Tennessee home town. So I've been asked, not necessarily by him, but others have asked me, not to disappoint people waiting for my brother Henry's service. Amen?"

"Amen," agreed a reassuring number throughout the congregation.

"Now I'm being followed by my beautiful daughter, Amanda, Miss Appalachia I might add, and carrying her guitar behind her is her helper Hardrock Adams. Just sit her over there, Hardrock, but a little bit farther back, if I may. That's good." He faced the increasing, as well as apparently increasingly restless, congregation. "I've asked Amanda to go through a couple of hymns to get us in the mood, then I'll say a few words, and those who feel led by the Spirit will handle some as the Bible mentions. Talking in unknown tongues definitely is a plus."

Elford looked toward Hardrock who, as if taking a hint, handed Amanda her guitar in her chair and then marched to the rear bench to become the bench's only occupant so far.

"Now please let me say this," Elford added. "I'm asking that handlers stray not too far from their cages and that Amanda's and my few words will be only from the platform. Amen, everybody?"

Reassuringly, there were more Amens.

"I'm thinking of Elder Hiram Slocum and the last time I heard him preach. More inspirational words of everlasting glory I don't know that I've ever heard. If Elder Slocum had been living in Jesus' time he very well might have been tapped for one of them twelve. So we include him in our prayers as he fought for his life there in Tennessee. One advantage of staying on the same wave length is that you know that Jesus knows that we don't brag just to make somebody feel good. Thank you again, Elder Hiram. I also can't wait to thank Elder Slocum for being so kind to suggest this wonderful new church, electric lights and all. As I've already said, his reward is great in Heaven. I appreciate that too, certainly."

Elford looked toward a tall slender man who appeared mighty comfortable on the front row.

"And of course everything about Elder Hiram Slocum of Tennessee goes too for the Reverend Ernest Beasley of West Virginia who is still on sabbatical leave and I mean does it in spades. I've known Ernest for nigh on three decades. And I'll tell you one thing, if I want somebody to preach my funeral, it's Ernest." Elford chuckled and held a restraining hand toward the West Virginia minister now on sabbatical leave. "Not now, Ernest. Certainly not now but I guess later."

Elford raised a tuning fork. "Daughter, let's give everyone the word." Elford tapped his tuning fork and began leading, "Tell me the story of Jesus. Write on my heart every word. Tell me the story most precious. Sweetest that ever was heard."

Elford lowered his tuning fork and positioned his palms toward the congregation in restraint. "Now, folks, again I really am going to make my introduction brief and closing. I just want to thank everybody for attending. We call ourselves a convention of snake-handling people because that's how we seem to be known. But some of our good ministers has got cans or jars of poison in with their snakes, and at least one good Reverend," Elford paused to glance toward Reverend Beasley, "I think Brother Ernest Beasley has at least one blow torch for fire. So as soon as one of us has got what it takes and whosoever gets slain in the Spirit, you'll know it. Praise the Lord."

Elford lifted his Bible. "We can never think to do enough or say it too strong. John 3:16. 'For God so loved the world, He gave his only begotten Son, that whosoever believeth in Him should not perish, but have everlasting life."

Other voices agreed, somewhat more loudly now and against an increasing sound of rattles right and left. Elford faced his daughter, "Amanda, give us one more favorite song if you please."

Amanda without looking at her hymnal promptly began playing and singing "When the Saints Go Marching In". It seemed that the spirit of God was beginning to manifest itself here tonight for certain. Faces began to brighten as their owners stood, their lights no longer hidden under a bushel, more and more worshipers reaching for the Spirit with arms uplifted, more and more holding snakes.

Suddenly Elder Ernest Beasley, on sabbatical from West Virginia, perhaps inspired by Elford's compliments, began singing and dancing toward the cages, in particular a large one toward the right end. Except that what he was singing had nothing to do with the hymn, "When the Saints Go Marching In" or any other recognizable tune. He made his way to the cage, in fact almost stumbled into it to the audible dislike of its occupant. But his action seemed to inspire others, and others sang louder toward the cages. Not everyone, however. Brother Elford put quite a bit more distance between himself and his pulpit.

Elder Beasley was first to unload his cage, an action that produced an approximate four-foot rattlesnake about as large as his arms. Or that is it did until Brother Beasley held it above him with both hands, a position that made it somehow look smaller.

"Elder Beasley has been bit seven times, by actual count, my beloved." Now worshipers were claiming more cages, lifting out timber rattlers and diamond backs and copperheads and also two jars labeled "poison." If as many as a hundred Americans have died from snake bites and liquid poison as reported, these snakes and jars visible tonight near the upper Mighty Risky should do nothing to diminish such figures.

Brother Elford's attention was drawn toward the back of the church, specifically out the back door across the back yard toward the Boost's truck parked sideways. It looked like people were falling. Except Hardrock. He was in the process of leaning forward and inspecting several bodies on the ground.

The sign on the truck was defaced. Amanda's name on the truck was badly smeared. In front of her name had been scribbled the "F" word.

Elford faced his daughter. "Let me have your guitar, sweet." Then to his congregation he explained, "Folks, I brought Hardrock here to help him out of trouble. Now he's in trouble here so I need to get him home. Not especially for his own sake but for people around him. Bye everybody." He accepted Amanda's guitar and led the way on the far right and out.

7

MISS APPALACHIA
Absolutely

Amanda Boost became "Miss Appalachia" soon after she befriended Hardrock. She and her father were at a Hazard, Kentucky, radio station when its manager showed why he was managing. "My broadcast station is sponsoring a beauty contest based on snapshots, and—Miss Boost—I'd like to enter you in the contest."

From nine hundred and sixty-nine entries the station selected Amanda as Miss Appalachia.

Although Brother Boost privately down-played his daughter's rise to fame, he mentioned it at each service. In fact, the good Brother ran out of notebook paper after he transcribed sermon entitled "Beauty is As Beauty Does." Watch out for them doesn's!

"Sometimes we have to trade with sinners"

her father told Amanda as they rattled across the Risky River on the wooden bridge at Burt Mines. "Meaning the Burt Mines commissary."

She nodded. "I guess their commissary would have everything."

Elford parked their truck—its front end aimed at the commissary. "I'll just be a moment, Miss Appalachia."

As Brother Boost paid for the pen, he noticed a stack of magazines beside the cash register, topped by a magazine entitled *SHOW IT ALL*. The magazine's cover showed what appeared to be a naked man and woman in a swimming pool. Or at least he hoped they were swimming. "Young Miss," he addressed the cashier. "Unless my eyesight has gotten bug-eyed again, filthy magazines like that are supposed to be kept under a counter somewhere, if anywhere."

"It's where Mr. Burt himself has ordered them stacked," she responded firmly.

"Not in my neck of the woods," Brother Boost declared. "Those folks don't have anything on at all."

She shrugged. "This is where he said display them."

Brother Boost hesitated, and then said, "I'd like to buy one. Understand, just to be used as evidence for Kentucky's porn law."

She shrugged again. "That's what he said."

"We'll see about that. How much is it?"

She smiled in triumph. "A dollar twenty-five."

"Why, that's more than your price for a fountain pen."

"That's the price."

"Hand it over quick, then…before it explodes. Here's my dollar twenty-five. I hope I know what I'm doing."

Reverend Boost turned the magazine over so that Amanda couldn't see, only to discover the same full-page picture on the back. He tossed the magazine into the back of their truck.

"So much for porn," he said as they drove off.

"Papa, what's wrong with that magazine?"

"There's nothing that Rod Burt won't fix when I guide him to it," he declared and meant it.

8

GARVEY
Mine Alone

Up near Free Fall, Kentucky, coal miner Henry Boost became a snake-handling preacher in a bar-room fight at Rosie's Place. Henry had stopped by Rosie's "to tickle a little coal" from his throat. Instead Henry almost danced his last jig after arguing with a "union-scab strikebreaker," Henry's words. Henry ended with a knife inserted at a true ninety-degree angle in his left lung. Henry's friend, Garvey Satterfield, was with him and heard him promise while sprawled on his back his intent to become a preacher, a snake-handling preacher in fact. It seemed somewhat appropriate, however. With snake-handling, like coal mining, you look death in the face.

Meanwhile, Hardrock needed money for Alabama. The Double Brothers mine hired him temporarily and teamed him with his stepfather's one-time miner friend Garvey Satterfield.

Garvey was known to be the only real friend of the young miner's stepfather and, in fact, he had been with him in Stuttsville at Rosie's Place when Henry danced his next to the last jig.

"I appreciate this job, but I don't appreciate this four foot ceiling," he told his veteran partner at the start of their first shift together. Claustrophobia had never been a problem for Hardrock as far back as he could remember, but appreciation of freedom of movement had.

"Though it's the only temporary job I could find. Aren't there mines around here where a person can stand up?"

Garvey took his time before answering. He lay prone on the grimy floor and shoved his pick forward. "Not around here there ain't." A little later he said, "Speaking of low ceilings, son. Don't be too careless with that battery strapped to your side. It's almost up on your back already."

"So what? It's not in my way."

"But its acid will sure be. You got any idea how long it will take 'em to find an extra car to take you out?"

"Not really." Hardrock felt beside him, moved the battery pack farther down against his waist, and then shoved his pick forward approximately even with the older miner's. It was yet another reason to quit.

"With that acid pouring into your back? Hour or more."

"I'll be careful. Don't they have things in this mine for accidents, like acid?"

"Baking soda. But it soon gets too much trouble to bring."

They continued chipping at the coal. When lunch time came and as they opened their lunch buckets, Garvey observed, "Can't dig it all in a day, son. Steady does it, but no race. Who packed your lunch?" Paper was over both their meals to protect from the mine dust.

"Ma did. Or I guess you could say I did. Ma pretty much stays busy with the school."

Garvey took a bite of some kind of sandwich. "What you got looks better than mine. I'll tell my old woman to straighten up and pack me something good."

Hardrock extended a slice of cornbread. "Here. I'm not really hungry. At least for the last part of it."

Garvey waved it aside. "Just like your old man, ain't you? Generous to a fault."

Hardrock looked aside. "What makes you say that?"

"Over at Stuttsville. I rushed to him when he took them cuts."

Hardrock's stare continued.

"Yep. Why do you think the bosses put me with you?"

"That's the reason? Because you were with him at that Stuttsville free-for-all?"

"Yep. Mighty good friends. He'd drink a little. Sure. He and I did a lot of that, I reckon, down the line."

Hardrock ate in silence for a while. "I've been wondering what really happened. I guess you knew him all right. He was generous and he drank."

"To a fault." Garvey enjoyed a sausage biscuit, his own. "In both ways." Garvey closed his lunch box without looking down, rested it on some nearby coal, lifted his pick, and after a little hesitation, resumed. But Garvey's arms weren't as strong as they once were. Without much effort the muscular Hardrock resumed chopping about twice as fast as his venerable partner.

Hardrock considered the problem and with it conjured a solution. Garvey, like many old miners, had established routines that involved concentrating on the coal seam in front of him rather than what was beside him. So each time Hardrock pulled back enough chunks of coal from the seam, he made sure that some of it rolled over onto Garvey's coal. When they weren't close enough to roll something onto Garvey's pile, Hardrock decided to choose a time and carry them there. He figured that Garvey must have noticed, though he never objected. After all, the new employee's efforts would have made Garvey look bad to the one or more foremen coming by every day.

Once Garvey said, "Hardrock, I seen what you did. Pushing coal in my direction time after time."

"I didn't want too big a pile to work with," Hardrock said.

Garvey gave him a knowing smile. "I understand, but your helping me that way made me think of your pop if he ever sobered up a little." Garvey groped into his grimy overall's pocket, and then finally reached around to grope with both hands because the object he was seeking was fairly large and cumbersome. After several failures and after pulling in his slender stomach, he dug out from the pocket an extra large pocket knife. "This is a frog-sticker," he said unnecessarily. Then for some reason his face looked red in the coal dust. "Yours," Garvey said at last with an audible sigh.

"Garvey, that isn't my knife. Pa never thought I was old enough to handle a big one."

"Not a kid. But now you're pushing six feet," Garvey sat down his lunch box and abruptly opened a red-tainted knife blade. "That's body blood," he said as if proud. "There was a fight and your pa put that knife between a miner's ribs without killing him."

Hardrock forced himself to look at it. "You weren't the person Pa stuck with the knife, were you, Garvey?"

"Oh no, your pa never turned on his friends. It

was the ones he didn't count as friends most likely to feel his steel."

"You can keep it."

"Not really, son. I didn't get it fair and square. I've been dreaming bad things about it ever since I done it." Garvey closed the knife and handed it to him. Without looking down, Hardrock let him push it into his hand. "It's not mine, Garvey. It's yours. Evidently he wanted you to have it, and that's why it's in your pocket, not mine."

"Not really. I took it off him and he hadn't been whopped ten minutes." Garvey sighed, as if relieved to confess. "Do you hear what I'm saying?"

"You stole it off him?"

"I stole it off him." Garvey sighed louder. "Everybody talked about him using that knife. Everybody wanted it, so I stole it."

"Garvey, you've sure made it all right by telling me what happened. If you insist, I'll take it. But I'd like to return it to you."

"No, I'd rather have the sleep, Hardrock. I'd rather have the sleep." Garvey lifted his pick and began chopping away. "Just promise me a prayer along the way if you will. When you look at it, think of me. I hope I'm still in the mine. I hope I'm still able to work in a mine."

Hardrock laughed. "That's the easiest bargain I've run into." He resumed chopping in earnest.

Garvey laughed, deeper than before. "I'm feeling good already. I really am." Garvey looked toward the dust and the grime guarding the coal seam, or maybe he saw the seam itself trying to hide. "Why not set fire and burn the coal right here?" Hardrock asked aloud. Yet underneath his banter lay an underlying tone of fear. Fear of the mines. The union at Double Brothers Mine had done much to make the mine safer, yet there was much to be done. Hardrock all his life had heard such dangers "cussed and discussed" and it was hard to be in any mine, Double Brothers, or otherwise, without thinking of breathing choking items that tasted like soot or smoke, or straining to see through eyes watered with irritation, or standing in shoes wet and cold or grasping pick handles that tended to resist like sandpaper.

He had heard for sure that more than a mile back in the mountain, though Garvey and he were dry for the present, there was an inch of water on both sides of the track. In some of the rooms past them water rose to men's knees, and now and then came sounds of sloshing nearby. They could hear shovelfuls of slag and coal filling empty cars, despite too much seepage still coming through the rocks, without enough ventilator fans yet in place to pull all the gas and the other bad air out.

Chunks of limestone still fell loose between overhead penning, causing more coal dust to threaten anything that breathed or tried to. But at least they were better off than some mines, where miners were being paid only a few dollars for an eight hour shift, most of it on their knees in places that featured bending rather than standing. Without enthusiasm Hardrock grabbed the air drill, leaned its weight as best he could against the coal seam, and the whole world seemed to vibrate as the bit lunged into the seam. Nearby Garvey continued picking at the coal in stride. The pick was certainly slower but lighter and at least some of the time didn't vibrate.

"I will say this in defense of Henry," Garvey said, "in respect for his memory here at Double Brothers, they ought to take that town called Stuttsville and blast it off the face of the earth. You know it's owned by Moe Stutts, who in turn is owned by any Burt who can breathe, starting with Rodney Burt, Sr., and Buckshot Burt, and down, if there is a down."

"I'm listening."

Garvey apparently didn't hear. "Don't turn your back toward any Burt you're about to meet, my young friend. They didn't get them mines by teaching Sunday school on mountainsides."

Hardrock was already crediting Garvey with much more than average intelligence—a Double Brothers' employee whose opinion really meant something. Garvey didn't seem the type to pass negative judgment unless the person really needed some.

"They sure lack friends here at Double Brothers," he agreed aloud.

Garvey gave him a direct look. "I guess you've heard how the Burt's got their start in the War Between the States."

"I heard Pa say once that back in the Civil War they'd sell something to anybody, North or South, and neither side liked it when it was to the other or something like that."

"If that something meant moonshine, you heard right as rain. The Confederates hanged one Burt—they claimed the proud parent of a half-dozen little Burts—for selling to the Union. He'd killed a dozen deer, crossed the Union line, and sold 'em to a bunch of Feds for meat. I reckon it wasn't for hides because you never hear of deer hides. That cooked the goose as far as the Rebels figured it, and they hung him from a peaceful weeping willow, people said, beside the Risky River."

Hardrock thought of the time he had failed to shoot a waiting deer and said nothing.

With a quick swing Garvey cut loose a large chunk of coal. "Then one or more Burts got to figuring that hauling around dead deer was maybe too much work or at least too easy to spot. So they started selling hooch, sometimes better known as moonshine, to both sides."

Garvey paused as a noisy string of coal cars came rumbling in from the mine opening about a mile east. The noise was increasing because the train would pass on the mainline track within about fifty feet. Also, the train was acting like a plunger, increasing the action of the in-flow and out-flow air ducts that opened in the room where he and Garvey worked. Not only the noise, but the dust in the air increased, and Garvey from habit remained silent lest talking he inhale more than necessary. After it rattled past, Garvey grasped his pick nearer its head to minimize the swing. He was thinking more and picking less. "What them Burts did was peddle hooch to both sides, if you can believe that. Now and then behind the lines on both sides giving 'moon songs' or 'moon whistles.' Get what I mean?"

"Listening."

"From the word moonshine. At night they'd set up shop on a log or in a clearing—not during battles of course. Then they'd sing or whistle words from "John Brown's Body" to sell the Feds, or "Dixie" to sell the Rebs."

Hardrock hesitated. "Sounds dangerous to me."

"If it was dangerous for the Burts, what about the troopers, Feds or Rebs? Say they hadn't tasted hooch in six months. To keep from getting ambushed when they visited 'the store,' they'd always come in two or more. So in case of a trick, like an ambush from the other side, they could prove that pranks don't pay."

"I was wondering about that."

"So when the war ended, a bunch of Burts,

people say, ended up with a bunch of Federal money. They also ended up with Confederate too, but the Confederate money wasn't worth a Yankee dime which, after the war, was worth twice as much as it was before."

Hardrock found himself tasting air to check its freshness. "Results weren't reassuring. I hear you."

Garvey had more news. "And so the Confederates didn't have enough to pay their taxes and that's when—I've heard—some Burts almost a hundred years ago started making good use of whiskey money."

"And I guess it wasn't much of a step from there to widows who are dying."

"Them Burts have always took the big step, no matter who or what. Big black horses with silver buttons on their saddlebags. First to own a car in the valley—make that a car and a pickup. Long vacations at the Gulf in winter. Boats almost as big as lakes."

"I'm impressed."

"I don't know if you ever visited Burt Mines, Hardrock, but talk about stamping your name. Burt Street instead of Main Street. Burt Subdivision when the whole town is named Burt anyway. Even Burts Church instead of First Baptist. Somebody asked 'what's in a name?' The answer is nothing, if it's a Burt."

9

FORGET ME NOT
Gone But Not Forgotten

Hardrock thought he saw the flash of a rifle high on the mountain overlooking the Risky and the Mountainside campus, that, plus Garvey's loving account of the Burt's long rapt sheet.

Shouldn't he do something meaningful before he left? He was approaching the school's gym building, and instead he veered left and began hiking alongside the Risky River's dirt road toward Burt Mines.

He saw approaching on the road across the Risky the Boost's truck. Amanda had said she planned to visit the bluff and make sketches for her amateur art class. The fact that he continued his visit to Burt Mines instead of detouring to meet Amanda highlighted the seriousness of his mission.

The river reminded him of those practice

sessions – hitting objects as they floated along. And the approaching river bluff reminded him of coal mine thugs standing – maybe — on it and firing on the Mountainside campus.

Upstream from the bluff the Burt Mines came into view. On the flat wooden bridge a coal truck partly filled suggested the company's need for coal.

Welcoming him was a large billboard sign that read BURT MINES, with the word BURT twice as large as the word MINES. At the two story headquarters building downstairs he entered the receptionist office.

"I'm here to see Mr. Rodney Burt," he said.

"Aren't we all," she retorted.

Hardrock felt his eyes narrow slightly. "The President, Mr. Rodney Burt. About some possibilities for coal."

"Mr. Burt meets only by appointment. You don't look like you have an appointment."

"It's a matter of life and death."

She stared. "You some kind of nut?"

He met her gaze until she reluctantly glanced toward the phone. Then after an appropriate sigh she dialed a number. "There's a man here asking to see Mr. Burt. He says Mr. Burt's life's in danger. Sounds kooky." She listened. "No, not exactly like that." Using her forefinger she coyly cleaned a little lipstick off the corner of her mouth and gave her visitor a sidelong glance. "In fact he's cute."

But her expression darkened as she listened further. She placed a hand over the phone and again looked at him. "I'm glad you can't hear his secretary. She's even worse than usual this morning."

"So am I."

The one with the troubled lipstick replaced the phone. "I guess he'll see you. I think that's what she says. She's upstairs in back." She yawned and nodded toward the stairs. "Upstairs. All the way up. I've seen some people go in there and never come down."

"Good. Have you considered glasses?"

Once you saw Burt's upstairs receptionist you sensed why she was upstairs and the other down. Also the dozen or so people applying for employment seemed appropriate to a man of such high standing.

"I'm Hardrock Adams," he told the receptionist. "I hate to move ahead of all those people out there in your waiting room, but this is a matter of life and death. And I do have to leave on an important trip."

"Oh, don't worry about those job hunters out there." Her smile increased. She deserved her upstairs employment. "Hardrock, is it? Well, they're all waiting to hand me some kind of job application." Then she leaned toward her computer and added past lips firmly painted. "But nobody's hired until I'm ready."

Her shadow, as she moved, played across the

name on the door glass to the inner office and behind that it's distant occupant. The sign read in huge letters ROD BURT PRESIDENT. But the figure in the swivel chair behind the desk with a phone to his ear looked too young to be heading a huge coal mining company.

"That's not Rod Burt the company President, is it?"

"No that's Roddy." She smiled. "Don't tell him I called him that. But his name's Roddy and mine's Shirley. That's his old man sitting at the desk with the phone in his hand. Roddy's helping out a little this summer I think. Then to Princeton this fall. He's a Princeton nominee or nominee Princeton, however you say it."

"I've seen him before."

"I knew all this even before he told me. His own father told me. By the way some people call his old man "hot" but I'd never do it."

"I might. Depending on how much he doesn't like it." Hardrock opened the door, stepped inside and closed the door behind him.

Buckshot Burt stood inside the office reading aloud to his father from a book entitled, as it turned out, "Best Gulf Fishing". On the wall behind father Burt a loaded rifle rack waited.

"That school holy roller," Buckshot cried to his father, lunging toward the rifle rack behind his father's desk.

Hardrock decided to help them both stay unarmed. As Buckshot landed with a grab toward the lowest rifle, Hardrock met him at the nearer end of the desk, and as Buckshot leaped toward the lowest rifle on the rack, Hardrock swung the lower part of his body toward the incoming orator, who crashed his head into a sleeping mode about halfway up the rifle rack.

"That school holy roller," father Burt emphasized. "He's yours, son, he's yours." The father followed his words by grabbing toward something in his middle desk drawer, and as Hardrock shoved the drawer on Burt's wrist, the president yelled a horrendous "Ei EE."

"If you can wiggle your fingers, it's not broken," Hardrock said.

"He's a holy roller." Burt repeated.

Or that is, almost repeated. Burt had the misfortune of almost jerking up a revolver. Hardrock jerked it up instead. "Now I'm going to slide this to the middle of the room. I'm leaving because I don't plan to hurt you anymore today. But stay away from Mountainside. Get your coal some place else."

"Sure," Burt said and with his good hand managed to pick up his phone. "Take care of this one real good," he said. "The works."

10

THE BLUFF
Mighty Risky

Hardrock had barely begun his return hike to the school when a Ford pickup labeled Burt Mines pulled even with him and stopped. The figure behind the wheel resembled an olive-tanned Rod Burt, plus about thirty pounds, and most of it not fat. "Offer you a ride up the road?" It sounded like a statement.

"Thanks just the same. I like the exercise."

"I said, could I offer you a ride up the road?" This time the would-be Good Samaritan reached up behind his shoulder and adjusted the rifle in its rack. The message was clear.

"Oh, why didn't you say so? I see what you mean."

"This truck's better armed than a godfather."

"Than a godfather?" Hardrock said. "Sure."

The driver was opening his front passenger door as Hardrock moved around to that side. That door also heralded the Burt Mines sign. After a glance at the driver Hardrock swung onto the seat. It seemed good that Burt Mines seemed so well displayed. Strike-breaking goons typically could frighten strikers with their appearance as well as their strength or firepower. This one reminded Hardrock of a mine explosion.

"It certainly is a nice day, isn't it? I'm Hardrock Adams. My father is a preacher and my mother is on the faculty at the school."

"Yeah. And I'm Frank Sinatra."

Hardrock grinned grimly. "You don't look like it. For one thing you maybe aren't quite as skinny." What he did have, though, suggested hard use as in punching bags. His neck and arms looked about as thick as his chest, which was huge. In fact he looked about as square as vertical. "What's your real name, brother?"

For a full minute or longer the other seemed engrossed altogether with his driving. Then he shook his head as if sobering from a punch. "I'm Frankie Sallio. Sounds like Frank Sinatra, don't it? I don't mind telling you my name, I guess, because your memory's about to leave you permanent." Sallio glanced mischievously aside. "Plus a lot of other things."

"A lot of other things? I don't understand."

"I guess I should explain I've got your

contract," the driver said.

Hardrock looked aside. "Contract...contract?"

"I have to kill you. I might as well tell you. Because when you go, what I tell you goes with you."

"I wasn't planning on going anywhere except down this road."

Sallio's laugh was not heartwarming. "It's fun for me—might not for you—to be able to talk when I can say anything because you can't tell."

"Are you saying contract like the Mafia?"

"Sure. Why not?"

"But you're not Mafia, are you?"

"I've got close relatives, though. In Chicago and New York. I've got a brother who's a priest, too, but he's not counted."

"What's the Mafia doing down here in this part of Kentucky?"

Again the driver laughed. And again it was not heartwarming. "I don't mind telling. Again it's a matter of you keeping your mouth shut."

"At one stretch I did a little time at some Pennsylvania coal mines. So they've made me an offer."

"To murder me?"

"Jack, Jill, you name it. Though murder's hardly the word. Since you're from that so-called church school they want it to look like an accident. Maybe falling off a bluff."

Hardrock's laugh was in the same vein. "What

if I don't want to fall off a bluff?"

"It's my job to help you make up your mind. Of course without getting my feet tangled with yours, or something like that, going over with you." The driver's laugh sounded deeper.

"I told you that talking like this is fun. Well, I don't mind your knowing I'm a great singer. All Italians sing, but I reckon I'm greater than anybody I ever heard. Want to hear me?"

This sounded a little better. Even almost friendly. "Sure, I'd love to. Or I think I would." Many things were worse than bad music.

"You rather I'd sing it base or tenor?"

Hardrock started. He couldn't imagine this hefty congregation of muscles singing tenor. "Why not? Let's hear tenor."

Sallio laughed. "So he wants tenor." Sallio glanced at himself in the mirror, and rounded his lips for a warm-up, "O." Then, "Moonlight is now for you. Moonlight is for you now. To you forever I'll always bow. You're like an angel. Not a sow."

Hardrock stifled a laugh. But that tune certainly wasn't as ominous as Sallio's rifle. Or his implied threat pertaining to other weaponry. "Surprisingly good," he agreed aloud.

Abruptly Sallio's expression hardened. "You wouldn't call a man a Dago, would you?"

Hardrock was pleased to be truthful. "Never have and never will."

"I'm a proud Italian, so I especially don't like

Dago. Grew up next to Jersey, working them Pennsylvania mines. If somebody knows you're Mafia, you sure get some respect you're entitled to."

Hardrock hesitated. "Fair enough."

"Sure. I'm coal mining Mafia. I don't work for the mob officially, but I do everything they do and better. We're all family."

"There's nothing wrong with a good family," Hardrock said for want of something better.

Sallio laughed, cleared his throat, and again burst into song, but this time his voice was a bass. "My baby likes muscles. And I like to muscle in. My baby gets impatient, if all I do is grin." He glanced aside at Hardrock. "All my blood family sings. All four of us. My two boys like me. They ain't as good as me, but they're good. Count on it."

"I'll bet they are." No pain, no strain.

"Or here's another one," Sallio said. "I dream of my love. While the stars shine above. I'll take off a glove to my very true love." Sallio laughed with pleasure. "I wrote some of 'em myself. I've copyrighted 'em all that I've wrote. Just waitin' for my chance."

"They're good," Hardrock said. Certainly better than the business end of a .22.

"Then here's my last." Sallio laughed in apparent anticipation. "I'll serenade you at the gate. But our love will bloom at a later date. My song to you is like fish bait. My love will never be too late." For good measure, as if dancing in a musical, he had his huge feet dance up and down against the floorboard.

Sallio looked left and began braking the pickup. "See that log lane peeling up the mountain?" He laughed lightly. "Let's find what's up there." He guided the pickup onto it, and as he did so his demeanor abruptly darkened. Apparently the journey, as well as his song and dance, was nearing an end. The lane continued rising for approximately fifty yards up barely navigable terrain, then ended at the first cliff overlooking the road and the Mighty Risky. An overgrown path, impassible for a vehicle, led higher up the mountainside.

"That one's easy. Call it live and let live."

"That's what you say. You just put a contract out on my boss in his own office." He turned onto the rocky plateau.

"A contract? You can't be serious. Me put a contract on Burt?"

"Every official I ever met is on the list with every organizer I never hope to meet. It's a kiss of death."

They were approaching the top of the bluff. Sallio applied brakes, slightly skidding the truck's tires. "Your best chance to come out of this alive— you've got no chance—but your best chance is step outside and do like I say. My rifle's easy and I'm holstered left." The bluff was about the size of an indoor firing range. "I've about talked out," the goon said, "Now get out."

"Why?"

"Because I can snatch this rifle faster than you can. Now out."

Hardrock frowned slightly. This at last was beginning to seem serious. "Frankie, you have a bad habit, at least it seems bad to me, of asking for something, and then explaining why. I now understand what you mean. Thanks." Obviously talk was still cheap. And he was still breathing. Hardrock stepped out.

Sallio climbed out on the other side, rifle in hand. But even more to the point, it was now quite obvious what he meant by his truck being armed like a godfather. And more recently by being "holstered left". Slapped on his left side was a dull brown holster waiting to cough up a large black revolver.

Their owner sounded off again. "Walk toward the edge. I'll only shoot if you start to run. But like I told you we don't like bullet holes. Knock you off this cliff. All the way down. Like an accident."

His captive really hesitated with this one. There had to be some advantage in having the truck between himself and firepower. But it was about the same advantage as a sitting duck, he decided. He walked slowly toward the bluff, his back to his captor.

After his captive's half dozen paces Sallio

called, "Far enough. Face me." As he spoke he balanced his rifle against the side of the truck, and then lifted a large coil of dynamite cord from the truck bed. Unraveling it he tossed the end toward Hardrock. "Tie it around your waist." Sallio took time to grunt and then laugh as he fumbled a little with the cord. Apparently sweat was beginning to make his small eyes more watery. "It's to your advantage to tie a good knot at your end."

Hardrock began complying. Sallio might be a lunatic, but at least he seemed to know how to package someone. As Hardrock tied the cord around his waist, Sallio took slack at his end and secured it to the truck. Apparently he wanted to keep his visitor in easy range. Then, grinning, he relieved the truck bed of a large coal shovel. "Show me how to dance," he called, holding the shovel like a spear. He lunged toward his captive, then pulled the shovel back just in time to keep from bowling Hardrock backwards and over the edge. Grinning, suddenly panting for breath, he almost squatted. "I said tell me which mine the UMW's targeting next?"

Hardrock complimented himself for not recoiling backward enough to break the cord and go sailing. He credited his feeling of courage, to his athletic ability. "I only worked a few weeks."

"You're United Mine Workers to the core."

Sallio thrust forward again. But this time Hardrock's right hand diverted the shovel down and aside. He thought the cord might break because the blow, though diverted, was enough to force him back a couple of feet nearer the edge behind him. The shovel's cold steel in his hand was not too cold to prevent a hot stab of pain from shooting toward his left shoulder. The blow caused his right hand to spring to life with blood, splattering it also up his arm. He had never realized that fresh blood had such a distinctive odor.

Sallio, obviously growing impatient, came thrusting in again, much faster than last time. Hardrock decided that with this third one his best bet was to grab the shovel with both hands, taking it squarely in his chest perhaps but in the process possibly unbalancing Sallio. Except that this time Sallio stopped several inches short of his target. He obviously was hoping to scare him into jumping backward. "This sure ain't gettin' us anywhere," called Sallio, his tone now definitely more bass. He grinned and looked toward Hardrock's feet. "Here I come," he cried, his grin widening. Holding the shovel like a javelin or spear he aimed toward Hardrock's feet, as if tapping for coal. Hardrock simultaneously spread his legs and jumped up. The shovel came down between and beneath his feet, scraping the rock, causing Hardrock to look like a dancer on sparks and cliff dust.

Sallio pulled back the shovel with a genuine sounding laugh. "You no talk. I no stop. The next one's higher." He again hoisted the shovel as might a sports competitor, or a tribesman, this time leaning forward in a sprinting position.

Suddenly a young woman's voice interrupted. "What are you doing? He's right at the edge." Approaching was Amanda Boost, with an artist sketch pad in her hands. At the moment her sketch pad was trembling slightly because of either the wind or her hand.

Sallio looked carefully back and forth from her to Hardrock then, unsurprisingly, attacked— leaping at her, giving his left hand the shovel, freeing his right to crush into the side of her head. She staggered back but did not completely lose her balance. Her half-completed sketch of the valley lay bent and twisted as if needing help.

Hardrock leaped forward and swung his right fist toward Sallio's chin, but Sallio turned in time to deflect the blow, instead swinging a vicious blow into Hardrock's stomach. Hardrock almost doubled and Sallio took the opportunity to release his shovel and grab his .45 from his belt. As he brought the gun out he slapped his free hand against Hardrock's shoulder, knocking the latter backward but in the process propelling himself nearer the edge of the bluff. As he did so Sallio dropped his revolver and it went scooting over the edge, leaving a trail of sparks and dust.

This time Hardrock's left hand reached Sallio with a blow that found a home between Sallio's throat and chin. But though the blow landed with a loud plop, resulting in Sallio's even louder grunt, and his small eyes watered more, Sallio after rocking back from the blow planted his feet again and at the same time hit Hardrock so viciously he was knocked back to within inches of the drop-off. Hardrock didn't see stars but his mind apparently didn't see anything else as it toyed with going completely blank. He fell forward and the same instinct that caused him to fall forward rather than backward also had him roll aside as he fell. Sallio lunged forward apparently to bowl Hardrock backward off the cliff, but with his captive rolling aside he instead landed on his own belly and now, like a surfer on a wave, he too came within inches of going over. Instead he wiggled around, like some huge animal, and then lunged toward Hardrock who was shaking his head and also staggering to his feet.

Amanda Boost ran to the pickup and groped in the glove compartment and then under the seat. She explained later that she would have used a weapon merely to frighten, not to harm, Sallio. Hardrock propelled a right to Sallio's stomach but the blow produced only a dull thud as if hitting a stationary boxing bag.

Sweat flowed more freely around Sallio's eyes but that seemed to be the only damage. Hardrock found his mind almost gone again. Except that he realized he not only was tasting blood, he now was smelling if not tasting death. All peaceful and quiet at last. For some reason he thought of his mother. Nearing peace at last. Or was it his father? Unwilling to go down. Strange how a blow to the stomach, if it's deep enough, causes you to taste blood.

It was Sallio's misfortune that he too misjudged the incoming left. It went counter to an enforcer's experience, if a survivor. Hardrock broke forcefully from his trance and retreated a partial step and at the same time his left fist widened Sallio's already wide nose. Sallio, coming in with his right, screamed, and his body shook as if in a cold shower which—according to Sallio's arm odors as he swung—he had avoided along with the heat.

Sallio screamed with pain and apparently inhaled blood into his nostrils. He now spat out red liquid, his chin reddened almost as much as his nose. But, as Hardrock's father had taught him for many, many years, it's not the punch and counter punch but the third one—the follow-through—that finally counts. He followed through in the direction of the cliff or—more specifically—in the direction of Frankie Sallio departing the cliff.

From ahead and below came a distant deep splash. But was it a splash or was it a Frankie Sallio song? Maybe something like, "Let me through that open gate. Do it your way. Just be my date." The body quickly surfaced three times and disappeared. Hardrock couldn't decide whether or not he was actually seeing blood in the water.

He tried to dismiss Sallio from his thoughts. Killing someone was a disappointing thing to have to do, but you must fight fire with fire. The Burts were known for their cold-blooded maneuvers. Blood starts hot before it turns cold. He sent a prayer over his shoulder asking that all go well with Sallio's soul.

"Are you hurt?" he asked as she turned from the vehicle.

"I'm all right. I think."

"Can you move your jaw? He hit you a rough one."

She felt her jaw. "I'm all right. Where is he?"

"Oh—the guy who planned to kill me? It was either him or me. Thanks again. You saved my life."

"How terrible for him. I'm sorry—I should have come earlier. I heard your voices and some scraping sounds. But it was a couple of minutes before I figured out that something was really wrong."

He let her inspect his hand. She frowned. "There's a cut behind you on your arm. Let me look at it to be sure."

"Sure, why not?" What a pleasure to smell someone so clean and fresh—rather than an unwashed Sallio, at least unwashed before his dive.

"That should be bandaged," she said. "I'll look in his glove compartment for first aid supplies."

"Sure why not", he responded.

"Nothing in here," she stated.

The rifle still leaned beside the truck, and the dynamite cord lay strung out over the rock. "How strange" she added.

"It's what happens when you offer someone a ride. You can never tell. They'll turn on you, maybe, like that man turned on me."

"Are you sure he's gone?"

"Oh yes. I'm sure."

Suddenly she stepped within a foot or so of the bluff's edge and looked down.

"What are you doing?" he asked.

"Seeing if he survived."

"That's too dangerous. Step back. As for that goon, who cares?"

"But if he fell maybe he's alive."

"Who needs him? I sure don't."

She looked aside with a forgiving smile. "Jesus said, 'Turn the other cheek.'"

"Amanda, please get back from the edge. Let me help look this way." He stepped aside, held onto a small pine, and looked over. He shrugged. "No sign of life. It's fifty feet down, five stories, and the road is packed hard. Though he probably ended in the river anyway, which really looks hungry, and I think I heard him splash, on landing."

"Well maybe he's trying to swim out."

"If he is, he's anywhere for the next several miles. After which he's in the Kentucky River, a few miles farther downstream than the school."

"I'd vote for going down and making sure," she said.

"Then let's. It's on our way back to school too, if you're headed that way."

"Yes, my father's expecting me within the hour."

"We can make it. We could ride, but when our enforcer arrived he slipped the truck keys into his pocket. He maybe had a premonition."

"I'm a little glad, anyway, we're not riding around in his truck."

When they arrived below, there was no sign of anyone, including Frankie Sallio. The river water looked deep and mysterious and anything but obstructed.

"He's either deep on the bottom or somewhere downstream," Hardrock observed. "There's no way anybody could survive that fall from the top." He pointed toward the bluff's edge, an action that visibly increased his arm's bleeding.

"That cut needs to be treated with first-aid. I'm sure they have it at the school."

11

THREE'S A CROWD
Unwelcome Bridge

At the campus they headed for the parsonage. Hardrock opened the porch door and held up his right arm. "See, the bleeding's stopped."

She smiled. "It won't take long."

"Who am I to argue?" He followed her across the porch to the office door.

"I'm sure you could handle it. I wonder where father is. He was looking for Reverend Hope."

Amanda knocked and a young girl with bright eyes opened the office door. "Thanks," Amanda said. "We need to speak to Sister Hope."

"She isn't here, ma-am. But I'll bet you know where she is. Yes-m. She's out helping with a baby. I think getting a new one."

"This man has a cut on his arm. Do you know where Sister Hope keeps her medical supplies for treating things like cut arms?"

"No ma-am. But Reverend Hope does. I think he went to the chapel to set up a meeting. I'm not sure but I think that's what I heard." Her bright eyes suggested no remorse for her eavesdropping. "I can run and get him for you."

Amanda reached down and patted the little girl's shoulder. "Thanks anyway but my dad was really looking forward to this meeting with Brother Hope."

Hardrock said, "I'll just go somewhere and wash it off."

"Here. Let me look at that arm again." Before he could object, even if he wished, she was holding his hand in hers. "It's just as I said. It's still a deep cut." She lowered his arm carefully.

"It seemed to feel better," he said. "Just your looking at it that way."

"I can even do better than that. I know what we should do now—I just remembered—a ready solution."

He said nothing. Even the little blonde was looking at his arm with a dismayed expression.

"I forgot our truck's medical kit. After I took that nursing course by mail. I think I have a first aid kit in our truck across the Risky." She glanced at Hardrock. "I think we'd better go."

"Sure, why not," he said.

Ahead of them across the river, parked near the end of the bridge, sat the truck with its words

BROTHER ELFORD BOOST AND HIS DAUGHTER AMANDA.

She laughed. "My Dad's always quoting that Bible verse about not hiding your light under a bushel. He believes in publicity and planning, in his words. That's why we stopped off here today."

"Planning on having a service here?"

"Oh yes. Papa just happened to notice a pornography magazine at the Burt Mines commissary. So he's started a statewide anti-pornography campaign. I think we're kicking it off here at Mountainside."

Hardrock said nothing.

"Not because of Mountainside, of course. But Burt Mines and Mountainside are close neighbors. Papa decided it would be more dramatic to kick off our campaign here."

"I guess so," Hardrock agreed.

"Oh, we've started it already. He just wanted to start it off with a big splash here at Mountainside."

She at least had the advertising vernacular down pat, he noted. Suddenly she reminded him of his lifelong question about luck. Why are so very few people so very attractive and so obviously intelligent with a great personality? Why do a very few people have all that given to them while the great majority have to fight for every rung on the ladder? Luck?

At the truck she hurried to the back, reached in

and moved a lever that lowered the tailgate, then pushed a second lever, this one lowering a couple of steel steps which she climbed with amazing ease. Then from forward on the truck bed she displayed triumphantly a shoebox-sized aluminum container. "Won't be long now," she called. "This should do it."

Her retrieving the kit happened so quickly he had barely reached the truck when she in turn came back and placed the kit on the side of the tailgate. She seemed to know where everything was in the kit because without hesitation her right hand brought out a bottle of alcohol and her left a bunch of cotton. Her hands certainly looked as sensitive and gentle as a nurse's. "Now," she said in a reassuring tone, "I'm doing everything Sister Hope could have done except a few minutes later."

"I'll buy that. At least so far so good."

"Now roll that sleeve high above your elbow, if you will, please. This will only sting a little. I've been taught to be very careful not to irritate the cut."

He rolled the sleeve high.

She indeed proved unusually careful, letting just the right amount of alcohol drop from the cotton as she rubbed. Then she dried it lightly with more cotton. "Now that doesn't hurt, does it?"

"Absolutely painless."

She smiled, replaced the alcohol and the cotton, and then brought out a bottle of iodine. "This will sting just a little but it won't last long."

He said nothing. Obviously what the world needed were a few more Amanda Boosts who had taken nursing by mail and a few less Frankie Sallios, for example. Though he hadn't produced any of the former he at least had lowered the Frankie Sallio count by one.

She was starting to cut the tape to secure the bandage over the wound, and he was reminding himself that he wished this bandaging could continue forever, when the bridge started rumbling loudly. It was rumbling loudly because a figure starting forward from the other side was doing so with unusually powerful strides. Responsible, or irresponsible, as the case might be, here came a tall, lanky middle-aged man. He looked like a somewhat younger Garvey. Except that this one looked at least a little more disturbed than even a coal miner should.

"That's father," Amanda answered Hardrock's unasked question. "That little girl must have told him we're here."

"Your bandage feels perfect, Amanda. Could I help you with that piece of tape?"

"No thanks. I have it."

"Well, it sure enough feels fine. Has anyone ever told you that you remind them of Florence Nightingale?"

"Not really." She smiled. "But thanks for starting such a list." She closed the kit.

He reached for it. "I'll take it back."

"Oh no. My father let's only me arrange things in the truck." She smiled wider and looked toward the bridge. "Speaking of Papa, yes, here he is."

Brother Boost must have heard her. Or perhaps in response to some medium he called. "Lucky for you it's your father, young lady. Some folks might take a different view of your cavorting across the countryside with a perfect stranger."

Hardrock laughed. "Would appreciate your emphasizing the word *perfect*, Brother Boost. " He extended his good left arm.

However, the swinging bridge was still rumbling from Brother Boost's determined passage. In this position he was unable to accept Hardrock's offer. "Daughter, I may be wrong, but I was under the impression that I told you, Sweetheart, how bad it is that we need to leave in an hour. I looked under every blade of grass on that campus, or almost, looking for you. Then I just happened to ask a little girl at the parsonage and she blurted out everything."

"Well what she told you is true, Papa. Even more than that, Mr. Adams here was attacked by a hitchhiker who badly injured his right arm. The girl told us that Sister Hope was away from the campus nursing someone, and that you were busy talking—or at least talking—with Brother Hope in the chapel. She didn't know where a medical kit was, and then I remembered the one I won—in our truck."

"I can assure you, Brother Boost," Hardrock said, "that everything was absolutely proper. That it happened exactly as she said."

"Oh that I am sure of, sir. My daughter and lies are two different things, sir. Never did and never will."

"And her memory is excellent."

"But, young sir, it's not her memory I'm worried about. It's my back. Or her back too. Here I turn my back for forty-five minutes and when I look around she's gone."

"Papa, I can assure you that absolutely nothing happened."

"Again, my child, it's what you mean by happened. I guess I'll have to tell this young man, after all, about the birds and bees, sweet." He faced their visitor. "You see, sir, a couple of months ago my daughter Amanda and I was across the Mighty Risky. We were heading back north from Burt Mines when I happened to stop by their commissary."

"I've already told him all that, Papa. Or the high points."

"Well I'm telling him the low points, dear. So when asked to pay, there by the register was some of the filthiest magazines you ever seen. When I asked about 'em they told me they're legal in the great and sovereign state of Kentucky."

"As we left, Papa laid on his horn and said it reminded him of money changers fleeing from the temple all right," Amanda added.

"Anyway, I checked in Frankfort and there ain't a law worth anything at all. So I'm going statewide. I already told 'em just outside Frankfort that if I don't get that law changed I'll give my daughter to Louisville vice."

Hardrock looked at Amanda. She was grinning, not smiling. He forced himself to keep from doing either.

"And so one final thing. My daughter is as pure as the driven snow, son. If she wasn't, them Louisville papers would make a statewide joke. So I'm keeping her clear of all kinds of men, two-handed or no-handed, or whatever, within grabbing distance of her, if you get what I mean."

"Even if they're about to die of gangrene poisoning, Brother Boost."

"I don't care if they're doing the rosary. I just want to be around when they're around. Is that clear?"

"As clear as that Mighty Risky behind you, Brother Boost."

"That's more like it." Brother Boost headed for the truck. "Let's go, dear. We're running late."

It was obvious that by "dear" he was only referring to one of them.

It seemed clear that in Brother Boost's household three definitely was a crowd.

12

THE CHASE
Who Has The Key

It was not Rodney Burt's day. First was Frankie Sallio. That was enough to convince him that Hardrock had to go. Company pride for one thing. You bring a coal miner like Frankie Sallio down from Pennsylvania, work through the rough edges, and then when he can be of most assistance some Holy Roller knocks him all the way from a bluff down into the Mighty Risky. Barricades usually work well. You barricade a road and you usually get someone, maybe even Hardrock. Word gets around. You're looking for or finding a suspect.

To get from Mountainside to Hazard meant driving south along the Risky through the heart of Burt Mining country. But Reverend Hope had a thought concerning this problem. He believed that the school car could make it through a roving barricade if anything could.

The car was available, and he too wanted to show the Boosts his support, especially for their anti-smut campaign.

Sister Hope from time to time drove through the area unharmed. She was a familiar widely-respected figure in her large white bonnet as she drove on medical errands of mercy, such as midwifery or first aid cases where doctors weren't present and practicing. She was as well known south of Mountainside as she was north, and anyone who tried to stop her would likely have foreshadowed his own first-aid need. Except that she had misplaced her familiar large bonnet, a matter of some concern as Hardrock drove away.

It was dusk as the Mountainside's car headed south on the road between the river and the mountain. Then suddenly, ominous in the distance, a number of men with rifles waited on the road.

Hardrock slammed his brakes so hard it dislodged Sister Hope's large bonnet—of all things— from the floor behind the driver's seat. Well, that bonnet was certainly no weapon, or was it?

He slowed the car to thirty-five miles an hour, which maybe could have been Sister Hope's familiar speed, and ended by grabbing the bonnet and swinging it to his head. He glanced again at his speedometer. He was still doing about thirty-five miles an hour, a speed that Sister Hope might be driving in an emergency. If he could continue at this speed, the miners could tell little if anything about the small portion of his face not covered by the bonnet. As for the bonnet itself, if they'd ever worn one they would probably have said forget it. At the same time he couldn't help but admire Sister Hope for having worn it.

He could count a dozen or more rifle-armed men loitering ahead on the side of the road. And then something else. Someone must have recognized the car because slowly all, or most everyone, started ambling aside. Their postures began to look more and more relaxed. After all, there weren't that many cars in the area, and the Mountainside Ford was easy to spot.

That is, all began ambling aside except one, a broad-shouldered miner with a surly grin that Hardrock believed he recognized as one of those miners in Rod Burt's waiting room. This nut, now holding his rifle in both hands not far above his head, stood there as if daring this oncoming driver not to stop. If he got hit without getting off a shot, there were still his dozen or more buddies to back him up.

Hardrock tried asking himself what Sister Hope would do, en route to an emergency. And then, why sure. She would honk and not slow, or not slow much, and manipulate her lights in this dusk. Well, he himself wouldn't slow at all. He began honking his horn persistently, turning his lights off and on, looking rigidly ahead as he continued.

Hardrock continued straight ahead at emergency speed, his face still camouflaged. And with several seconds to spare, the valiant miner stepped aside, out of the way. Hardrock kept sounding his horn and blinking his lights a couple of miles down the road. Then he set the bonnet gently on the seat beside him, comfortably.

He asked directions at a dilapidated store east of Hazard and in about three miles reached, as directed, a small church. It was about eight o'clock, well past sunset, as a bright naked bulb beamed its glaring welcome over the entrance. Parked in the church's small gravel yard were the Boost's makeshift truck, about a half dozen cars, two pickups, and four horses or mules. The animals waited in the shadows tied to nearby tree limbs. All church windows were open letting the strong spring breeze flow in to meet the stirring notes of "Onward Christian Soldiers." He looked expectantly toward the window between him and the pulpit. Though she, of course, was accompanying singing with her guitar, did or did not her cherubic face glance aside just then out through the window and on out to him?

But now abruptly Hardrock's thoughts returned to earth to a car parked farthest from the front entrance. The vehicle looked like a duplicate of several unmarked cars he'd seen at the Burt Mines.

But worse, there was just enough light from the bulb at the entrance to illuminate the driver's upper body. It was not a good discovery. Burt must have called an enforcer meet. So here then was another enforcer or enforcers.

Hardrock parked slowly a dozen yards from the light, keeping his door closed. The suspect driver slowly shoved an arm out his window and then abruptly made a violent swing of his arm upward, clearly trying to order the new arrival to come to him. Hardrock sat still.

The man pulled in his arm, turned briefly to his partner, then stepped out and pointed a rifle at the new arrival, motioning as if demanding his departure. He pointed with authority, as indeed he should. Their target must be the Reverend Boost's anti-smut campaign. Also, the Boosts were connected to Mountainside School.

Hardrock opened his driver's side door. He didn't believe the man would fire standing next to a church with open windows. Hardrock himself must do something. He hated bloodshed but the Burt Mines needed to remember that crime doesn't pay.

The rifle bearer began to advance. He was about six and a half feet tall and lanky, mindful of a number of mountain males, his right hand carrying a rifle and his left a large, unlighted stick of dynamite. He crunched gravel under his feet so loudly it sounded like pine cones or unlucky nuts.

He obviously meant business. Hardrock opened his door carefully and stepped outside, waiting within haymaker distance if necessary. The approaching warrior stared at him with a leer as he continued his slow, swaggering advance. Except that his stare, like an animal's, stayed on his victim; like an animal he too was trying to intimidate. He halted about six safe feet short of his prey.

"Afraid to come any closer?" Hardrock asked, speaking low. "Afraid I'll grab that rifle?"

"Afeered of what, you?" The tall man chuckled. "I'm walking you to my car to kill you." From his tall height he glanced aside at the church. "Where they won't hear you." He gave a low laugh, and then took another step forward. The man's eyes, at that, were too mindful of an animal's. Too close together and too piercing.

"Just one step? Is that all? You really are afraid of me."

As might a prodded animal, the man took a short step forward. However, his short step was not short enough. Hardrock took a full step ahead and announced his arrival. Too bad Frankie Sallio wasn't here to warn his comrade about that extra introduction. As the man staggered, Hardrock accepted his rifle. He jerked the rifle into a welcoming position and then his unoccupied left hand relieved the man of his dynamite. As Hardrock pulled back his knee, he said, "Please help me keep my temper better."

Meanwhile the late dynamiter seemed to be doing his own version of pleading. Except that in his case, he was simultaneously trying to regain his balance.

Hardrock shoved the dynamite into his left pocket and then tested the hardness of the man's back with the tip of the rifle. "Just walk forward slowly toward your car. That singing will drown it if I shoot you. March like they're singing, 'I Want To Be In That Number, When The Saints Go Marching In.' Put a little spring in that step, son, a little spring in that step." It sure felt good to short-circuit a potential bomb thrower, without whom the world would be better off. The world might owe him one for this one.

For whatever reason, perhaps the sound of the song, the feel of the rifle, the words of advice, or his physical pain, the man slowly moved forward. Keeping the rifle in touch with his captive was no easy task, especially as Hardrock himself tried to keep from stumbling on the gravel. One stumble and his trigger finger might react incorrectly, or correctly, depending upon how well the terrorist was liked by his family.

Now his buddy swung out and abruptly targeted Hardrock, pistol leveled over his car roof. "Another step, good-looking. You're dead."

Hardrock laughed as he stepped a little more behind his human shield and at the same time continued prodding the tall shield forward. "You want to kill your buddy?" he called to the armed one. "He falls, I shoot you."

"Not if I hit you first."

Hardrock laughed and called, still from behind his tall prisoner. "Open that passenger door real slow. Get in. Or I shoot High-Pockets, then you."

The pistol wielder hesitated, and then asked slowly, "How will you treat us in the car?"

"I'm putting you there for your own good. Painless." He and his prisoner were now less than a dozen feet from the car. "Move," he told his more-or-less walking companion.

The late arrival at the car debated a short time, lowered his pistol and then himself, reluctantly, onto the passenger seat, the pistol still aimed generally in Hardrock's direction, however.

"Okay, high-pockets. Now step forward and swing in under the wheel beside your friend. I don't plan to open the car door for you. Open it yourself."

The tall one put his left hand on the door handle, his right hand starting toward his body and then stopping. He spoke over his shoulder, "I remember you now. You're gone."

Hardrock grinned. "Inside."

Slim climbed in under the wheel and slammed the door hard between him and his unfriendly captor. Hardrock grabbed the rear door handle behind the driver and, rifle still in hand, occupied the rear seat behind the two. "Relax. Let's drive up the mountain."

"What?" the big one demanded.

"He's crazy," the fellow terrorist blurted.

Hardrock slammed the rear door, then just in case removed the dynamite stick and laid it on the seat at his side and then aimed the rifle between the two front seat passengers and in the same motion pulled the trigger. The shot in the closed car sounded like dynamite in a fragile mine seam. Or even dynamite inside a fragile car. The bullet penetrated the front seat and then the windshield, about evenly between the driver and the passenger, severing quite a bit more seat fabric than windshield glass. Both men grabbed their ears, though it was too late. But it was enough for the driver, anyway, to send a message. "I'm deaf!"

"Start this car!" cried his partner. "I said he's crazy."

Hardrock answered with a low laugh that probably did little to dispel this opinion. Then he grunted. "Drive out to the road and head up."

"Sure."

Driving up the mountain was dangerous itself. The curves were hairpin, the ascent too steep, the thick foliage ominous—nothing indicating what was right in the world, except containment of the two on the front seat. Also, one could be thankful for the variety of life, in his case, the continued taste of refreshing mountain air through the hole in the car's windshield.

After a couple of minutes, the driver asked in a low voice, hesitantly, as if afraid to hear an answer, "What do you plan to do?"

"How far since we left the church?"

The driver looked aside. "How far, Odell?"

"How should I know," Odell answered bitterly. "I ain't been here before either."

"Maybe six miles," the driver ventured, speaking slowly as if his answer might mean something.

"There's bound to be a wide place in this road up here somewhere," Hardrock said. "But with no traffic I can try turning around somewhere in the middle of the road. So brake it."

The driver hesitated as if debating the request, then abruptly complied, so much so they skidded partly sideways the last few yards before halting.

"Get out," Hardrock ordered. "While you still can." He eased the rifle against the back of the driver's head. The driver jerked open his door and in the same motion his feet hit the road and he began putting distance up the mountainside between himself and his late captor. His late companion, also clearly a fast learner, duplicated the escape on the right, except that he went crashing down the mountainside. Both rushed away like animals released into the wild by a benevolent hunter. Hardrock felt benevolent, all right; he had always favored animal rights. "Thanks," he said aloud. "Good riddance."

He swung out and then positioned himself behind the steering wheel. It required a half-dozen maneuvers, but he finally turned the car around on the narrow road. Except for the bullet-punc-tured windshield, it was not a bad return down the mountainside, either. In fact, the increased circu-lation of chilly mountain air felt refreshing. He even felt good as he considered the fleeting thought that there might be a need to patent the idea of a hyperventilated windshield such as this one. He thought of the car's former occupants scrambling across the mountainside and laughed grimly. Thanks to his father's advice, no benevo-lent hunter had turned them loose, just a righter of earthly wrongs.

Hardrock's return to the church was almost too late. Apparently collection had been had and the meeting dismissed. The Boosts' truck was begin-ning to look lonely with only a half dozen parish-ioners remaining to shake hands with their brother. Hardrock entered the church.

Brother Boost reacted first. "Of all things these mountains begat."

At Brother Boost's reception Hardrock, some-what taken aback, replied, "Brother Boost, thank you for the warm greeting."

"Warm or hot, as the case might be, Hardrock. We was just leaving. What brings you up to these parts?"

"Well, for one thing, I heard that you and Amanda were here. So I thought I'd stop by. Maybe help you with that truck driving, if needed."

"Well, I'm not sure I have all that drawing

power myself. Hardrock, these good folks still here should know I don't do solo. Me driving that truck without Amanda would be like washing your feet with your socks on, as they say. But I will say this, if you want to follow us, that's of course up to you. Driving a truck as old as that one, you might go belly-up any time."

"Then so be it," Hardrock said, "but slowly," and looked straight at Amanda. "So be it," he repeated.

"Oh yes, Hardrock," Amanda responded. "That would be a lot of fun, wouldn't it?"

"It's what you mean by fun," her father interjected. "If you mean riding behind a ten year old truck thirty miles off this mountain beside the Risky's fun, so be it."

Hardrock laughed. "So be it, Brother Boost."

Nor was it fun, Hardrock concluded, following their truck alongside the Risky. Maybe after they arrived at home, things would improve.

But as Brother Boost turned right onto their log lane, he no longer led the way. Instead he braked to an abrupt halt, opened his window, swung out his left arm, and motioned for Hardrock to pass by full speed ahead beside the Risky.

Hardrock decided he could take a hint.

13

A HAND FULL OF BURTS
Low Five

Obviously Amanda's father, Brother Elford Boost, appreciated help from his daughter's suitor Hardrock Adams. Especially in the wake of Brother Boost's inhibiting accident while changing his truck's rear tires. Brother Boost asked the potential son-in-law to participate in an anti-porn revival at the Mountainside chapel, denouncing the Kentucky state government before burning a porn magazine at the chapel door. Hardrock's help was even more needed because Brother Elford was giving the revival with a broken leg and two crutches.

For some reason, as Brother Boost explained later, he felt as if he'd just crossed the River Jordan. Planting his crutches on firm ground at the end of the swinging bridge he accepted, but with royal aloofness, his daughter's right hand at-tempting to help with his left crutch and Hardrock's left with his right. All of which caused the brother to add, "I feel like a three-legged frog walking this way, Hardrock."

"I'm glad you're sounding more like your usual self, Brother Boost. With that in mind I need to slip over to the faculty dorm for that magazine I'm to burn. I thought I'd have plenty of time to get it but it's still in my room."

"Oh yes," Amanda said. "You can walk without his help can't you, Papa?"

"Better, I'd have to say. With him lifting up at the same time you're pulling down, Daughter, I feel like a fish swimming backward down a wa-terfall."

Hardrock's laugh was brief. "Then I'll leave him with you, Amanda."

"Everything will be fine," she reassured him. "The important thing now is that magazine."

At the chapel she stayed beside her father as he hobbled into the building and down the aisle to the platform, perhaps an impaired announcer entering a ring. But before Amanda could move a chair to him, a Mountainside student hopped onto the platform and positioned one beside the pulpit, facing the audience as the brother approved.

"Folks," the brother began, standing awk-wardly in front of his chair, smiling back and forth between the daughter and the congregation.

"We're highly privileged to have with us today one of the truly great musical talents of our time, shall we say? The one and only, my beautiful daughter, the talented Amanda Boost, or Miss Appalachia, if you wish. Now let's give her a big hand, what do you say? A big hand."

There was applause and cries of hallelujah and amen.

"Now, Amanda," her father said, "how about getting that guitar ready for a little business, entangling it from that beautiful body of yours? And getting it ready for some good old-fashioned musical bliss?"

As Amanda readied her guitar into position, her father interjected, "Now for all intents and purposes, good folks, our number one attraction here today is my beautiful daughter herself. Hardrock here offered to help with my anti-smut campaign. He's about to burn a porno magazine. He himself will burn it."

Amanda raised her guitar, obviously ready to play.

"All right, Daughter. Let's start with this one, Sweet. 'Tis So Great To Trust In Jesus, Just To Take Him At His Word."

"Certainly, Papa."

"Amen," someone cried even before she began the first chord.

Brother Boost's left hand awkwardly found the back of his chair, but he faced forward again and there was nothing awkward about his right hand leading the congregation in the singing that followed. "Jesus, Jesus, precious Jesus. Oh for grace to trust Him more."

The brother managed to continue standing with his crutches under both arms and at the same time brush his face with his left hand. "Ain't that wonderful? Ain't that simply wonderful? All right, Daughter. Let's grab a chunk and sing like we mean it, 'When The Roll Is Called Up Yonder.' When the trumpet of the Lord shall sound and time shall be no more and the morning breaks eternal bright and fair.'"

Amanda swung into this as if indeed to grab a chunk, singing the words and playing the guitar without written music.

During the "Roll" Hardrock arrived, a manila envelope in hand. Meanwhile, the brother continued leading the singing with his right hand as his left somehow found the back of his strait-backed chair which he propelled toward Hardrock. "That chair's for Hardrock till the singing's over," the brother told him with a brotherly smile. To make sure Hardrock got the message he positioned the chair abruptly in the former's path as he faced it toward the congregation. Hardrock, accepted.

Brother Boost nodded briefly toward the halted Hardrock, and then smiled broadly toward his daughter. "But, sweet, we've got to have at least one more before Hardrock says his few words and burns that magazine. 'There Shall Be Showers Of Blessing.' How does that tickle your ears?"

"Surely, Papa." She began playing and singing, her enthusiastic congregation joining. "There shall be showers of blessing. This is the promise of love. There shall be seasons refreshing. Sent from the Savior above."

When it was over, the brother turned to Hardrock. "Okay, you. It's time for your few words, I guess."

If taken aback by the brother's brevity, Hardrock failed to show it. Instead he stood up, smiled toward Amanda, then her father, and finally his bread-and-butter congregation. He rocked a little on his feet. "I've been studying a little about politics. Folks, it's good to be here. To represent us forgotten people in this great and sovereign state of Kentucky. If we don't protect ourselves, who will? Not those pointy-headed big-government, big houses, big cars liberals in Louisville, and Frankfort, and Lexington."

Here at Mountainside there were cries and clapping.

"Raising taxes and keeping it there. They don't even know we exist. Collecting taxes—sure. Returning our tax money—not when they spend it on those Louisville skyscrapers."

"Never," cried someone loudly.

"They don't think like we do. They don't eat like we do. They don't sleep like we do. They sure don't sleep like we do. Which brings us back to porn. They're selling smut all over Louisville, and Frankfort, and Lexington. Our public libraries and our school libraries are yelling censors. They claim it's art. What do they want? Sex on every billboard in the great and sovereign state of Kentucky? And simply call it art?"

A thin elderly lady thought this was good. Her shrill voice was heard above those around her. "Never, never," she cried.

"It's not just big cities. Right next door at Burt Mines they're making money selling smut. They claim they're branching out, putting porn everywhere."

Many clapped loudly. Hardrock smiled at Amanda. "Very wonderful music."

"Thanks." He saw in this one his best opportunity yet to influence her father. If it called for stereotyped politics, so be it.

Hardrock continued smiling toward her for several seconds, then again faced the congregation. "Well I'll tell you what I'm going to do." He lifted the manila envelope. "I'm going to burn this porno magazine. Right there in the church house door. Those big-city pointy heads in Louisville and Frankfort and Lexington may be making money with our clean-cut children, but over my dead body they will."

He waved the envelope defiantly over the pulpit. "Let's follow me to the church house steps.

We'll burn smut yesterday. We'll burn smut today. We'll burn smut forever." He muttered aside to Brother Boost, "Take your time, brother. No use pushing it." With envelope held high he began strutting down the aisle as others rose to follow. Everyone was exiting without delay except Amanda and her father, being helped by his daughter.

At the door Hardrock took a couple of steps outside, turned, and requested, "Everyone outside to see this. Now who's got a match?"

As Hardrock prepared for his conflagration, a car with no lights but with two men aboard alongside the Risky was approaching the school. Probably the car wasn't approaching with occupants for the meeting, though their attire did feature suits and hats. Then the one on the passenger side took a chance by striking a match for his cigarette. The ignited match also revealed the two men's identity. Behind the wheel sat Rodney Burt's personal guard Rick Blades, his broad shoulders commandeering about half the width of the car. Beside Rick rode underling guard Joe Crouch who sat more than ready to take care of his half.

"It'd be nice if they'd hand us that Hardrock feller too," Joe said. "Get it all done at the same time."

"I don't see any sign of life," Rick said. "When I was growing up, they'd of had to use a baseball bat to get us to a church service."

"Here's the school sign. I'll duck this cigarette. No use taking chances."

"Right along here is where Frankie got it. On his way to have a friendly little chat with that crazy mad man who calls himself Hardrock. The language ain't got no words for how I see him."

"I still think the boss could let us take him here at school. The way he threw that dynamite and rifle and keys off that mountain like a mad man. Kept two of our best men walking all night long."

"We'll get him. He can't stay holed up in here forever. I'll toss him live off the bluff, straight down into the Risky. Talk about Frankie."

"The chief said the way Frankie got caught in those limbs down on the bottom he had to have dropped himself straight down. Couldn't have floated downstream into it."

"Hear that bellyaching over at that church chapel? I'm cuttin' back on my throttle just in case. There's no way they're going to know we found that parsonage."

"I hope I didn't duck it too early. I sure could use my smoke. You sure that safe's in his office?"

"All I know is that someone, who's almost as crazy as Hardrock and who someone claimed he bailed out of Eddyville says this. Says he saw a safe in the Mountainside parsonage that reminded him of someone's office. I imagine someone was joyed to hear that he was so much interested in the safe in his office, and that's for sure." Rick cut his engine and they coasted the last minute or so to the parsonage.

There was a light over the door to the screen porch and also a light inside. "The light's okay," Rick said. "They'd leave a couple on just to fool people. But you go around that way and I'll go this way and let's see if we can see anybody through the windows."

They met at the back at the office window. "See what I see?" Joe asked. A boy, aged about ten, slept on a pallet on the office floor across the room from the desk and a safe beside it. "Burt says that ever so often they sleep kids afraid of their parents."

"We'll have to waste him," Joe said. "Can't have no witnesses."

"Maybe he'll sleep through it," Rick said. "It's inside now or never. I want those clicks to open that safe."

They rushed around to the screen porch and into the office, the boy staying on his stomach as Joe began clicking the safe dial. It was a cheap safe and Joe didn't have to work the dial much to force the door open. "Hey, Rick, easy" Joe said. "Here's where it is—see what I've got?"

"Just getting some tape out of that old woman's handbag, or what she calls it. Case he wakes up."

"If we find it, we won't have time to tie him, will

we?" Joe asked. "Come look. Burt says the word at the top says DEED."

Rick stepped to him and quickly began shuffling the stack of papers. He pulled out one and held it up. "Right on the ball, Joe. I can read the word DEED. Those years in the joint didn't hurt your fingertips. All right, put the other crap back in and close it."

With the other material back in the safe and the door shut Joe turned to Tommy.

"Hey, what you doing?" Rick demanded.

"The boy moved. Dead men, in this case dead boys, don't tell tales."

"Back off, Joe. I don't need a murder rap for a boy if I don't have to. Here, that's why I got these damn bandages." He dumped Sister Hope's handbag onto the floor, releasing the odor of various kinds of medicines. As he brushed Joe aside, he began unwinding the largest roll of adhesive tape. "Burt himself says bring that deed in case some other nut also has Mountainside in mind." He stuffed the deed into his pant's pocket.

Tommy rolled onto his back and Rick pinned his chest down with a knee and with both hands otherwise free transferred a small section of tape to Tommy's mouth. Tommy began flailing his arms and kicking wildly up and out with his legs. "Wrap that tape around his legs. I'll tighten this bandage across his mouth." Tommy's attempted scream was nipped as it surfaced. "Now stop kicking," Rick demanded. He pushed more heavily with his knee, and as the boy began gasping for air he added some more tape to his mouth.

Joe grabbed both Tommy's ankles and wrapped the last roll of tape around them. "I told you the best way is waste him," Joe said, his breathing increasing as he struggled to capture Tommy's left ankle. Successful after a half dozen misses Joe straightened.

"Got both his ankles?" Rick asked.

"Yeah, but have you got his mouth and eyes?"

"Yep. Son, I'm dragging you across the floor like a dead hog, but if you don't scream you'll live. Here—I'm wrapping your ankles to this desk leg." Rick turned to his co-conspirator. "By the time we burn that girls' dormitory building we'll be gone before he squeals. I'll get our gas from the car. You just be sure you saved at least one match." Rick gave Tommy a parting look. "If you work that gag down and start screaming, we'll throw you in that fire and then in the river."

So flames started shooting up from the burning girls' dorm at about the same time Hardrock was setting fire to the pornographic magazine at the chapel door. One moment he was surrounded by curious observers, the next everyone was racing across the campus toward the burning dorm. Or, that is, almost everyone. Brother Boost, with his daughter beside him, was trying to join the rush but the tip of his left crutch got tangled in a clump of grass and he would have sprawled face forward except for her. She held his left arm as he regained his balance. "Papa, are you all right now?"

"It's what you mean by all right, Daughter," he answered, trying to catch his breath. "If you mean running around like a baby, the answer's no. If you mean almost breaking your neck on a crutch except for your daughter, the answer's yes." He resumed forward movement, but cautiously, with her continuing to hold his arm.

Suddenly Reverend Hope looked back, and seeing the Boosts' difficulty he hurried back. "Amanda, you're faster than I am. Run to the dorm and see if you can help. I'll bring your father."

"Certainly." Without giving her father time to object, if so he wanted, she hurried to catch the crowd headed toward the fire. As she ran she remembered some empty pails near the parsonage garden, good for rushing water up from the Risky. Also, there had been one or more hoes and a rake that might help salvage something.

The dorm was burning throughout the building. "Find something to bring water from the Risky," someone yelled. "It's too late," yelled another. "At least we'll try," cried someone else. Many students as well as faculty members raided the kitchen and dining hall for appropriate containers.

Several girl classmates asked to help Amanda in a water brigade from the river, to which she agreed, standing almost knee deep in water as she helped keep the little fire brigade supplied.

The Mountainside effort to save its dorm was the most spectacular event in its first thirty years except the flood. Before the dorm fire had claimed essentially everything, a dozen or more lines of water groups had formed between the Risky and the Risky side of the dorm. Between those lines, faculty members and students working independently were rushing up with full containers and down with empty. All were defying the devastating heat as if they dared it to try and stop them. Frank Hammer and his wife were individually lugging pails garnered from somewhere. Faculty poet Percival Rollins was lugging a dish pan for some reason while vocally lamenting his losses. "All my writing, all my life is burning in that inferno. Even my college diploma." He failed to explain why his material was in the girls' dorm.

Hardrock testified later that a student at the door to the boys' dorm handed him two waste baskets, and he rushed them to the Risky. Heat from the conflagration was reaching past the river's edge and the normally cold water seemed surprisingly warm as he scooped it into the containers. While he struggled for breath in the heat and flames, he had the strange impression that he was smelling a guitar burning.

He had tossed fresh containers of water onto the burning dorm and was hurrying back to the river for more when a student came rushing toward him from the direction of the parsonage. Reverend Hope was calling out for everyone to be careful of the increasing flames and falling debris, so Hardrock at first did not hear what the student was calling. The student was little Becky Judd, a fifth grader, who was running toward him amid all the chaos.

"Tommy's hurt," she said approaching Hardrock. "Something's wrong."

"Where?"

"In the preacher's house."

"Parsonage?"

"Yes."

Hardrock looked at what was left of the ill-fated building, for some reason reminding him of a burning guitar. Reverend Hope had arrived with Brother Boost and was warning those who would listen to stay far away from the little that still stood. Amanda, with her little crew, was still valiantly transferring water up from the river.

"Show me," Hardrock said to Becky and followed her to the parsonage office door where he stopped abruptly. The office looked like it had barely survived a flood or fire, and there on the floor lay the student Tommy Littlefield. Not only on the floor but apparently bound to a desk leg.

"What's wrong, Tommy? Are you hurt?"

Tommy may have cried, true enough earlier in the parsonage, but his voice now was as steady as an expert on a witness stand. "When Mrs. McFarland threw me out of that kitchen, Reverend Hope said I could catch up on my sleep in his office. That's when those two men broke in."

"Are you hurt?"

"No. Just my feelings. They put the hurt on Reverend Hope's safe, though—they were looking for Reverend Hope's safe sounded like. That's when I think they saw me move."

"Well, don't move now. I'm trying to free your feet that are really wrapped."

"It feels like you know what you're doing," Tommy said.

"At least your ankles are not too swollen." It reminded him of Amanda's medical help at the swinging bridge.

Becky said, "I came in for a waste basket. And I see it. Can I take it now?"

"Yes," Hardrock said. "The dorm is about burned down. But you might as well." He said to Tommy, "Some of your bandages are caught on the desk leg. Try to stand up as I lift a corner." Tommy proved more than ready to rise however wobbly.

"Tommy, that's more like it. Now, did you hear any names when they thought you were asleep?"

"Oh yes sir," Tommy said at once. "I thought maybe you'd ask. I must have memorized them a hundred times. Rick, Joe, and Burt. I remembered them a hundred times."

"That's terrific, Tommy. Now I'm going to lift the desk leg enough for you to free your other ankle. Are you ready?" Hardrock gripped the desk's guilty corner.

"Never been more ready in my life, Mr. Hardrock. As soon as you lift I'll jerk my ankle."

"Fine." Hardrock lifted enough for Tommy to jerk free of the desk, then lifted him by the waist. "I'm going to set you in the Reverend's chair while I take these wrappings from your wrists. Here we go."

"I hope so."

"There's probably fingerprints on something around here. Will you warn people not to handle anything?"

"Because of...sure I can, Mr. Hardrock."

Hardrock stepped to the phone and dialed the operator. "I need to speak to the FBI in Hazard." Both unions and non-unions had requested FBI clout in the area, the non-unions to prove foreign influence in the UMW and the UMW to prove lack of same. It became one of Hazard's most-called numbers.

There were several clicks and a male voice answered, "FBI."

"I'm calling from Mountainside School at Free Fall. The girls' dorm has been torched and one of the students kidnapped and bound to a desk. It follows fighting in the Coal Mine War, in which you're still interested, and it looks like fingerprints all over the place."

"All right. We're on our way."

"Good," Hardrock said and how he meant it. "Let me meet you with one or more 'torch boys' at the highway end of the school's swinging bridge."

"We'll be there. Leave it to us."

"Good." He dialed the number he remembered for Burt Mines, then discussed with the operator the possible whereabouts of Rick Blades and Joe Crouch and possibly Rodney Burt, Sr. He thanked her for being helpful and as he hurried out he gave Tommy a smile of encouragement with the words "Hang in there," then hastened his pace.

He was not fearful of being noticed tonight outside on the Mountainside campus. Everyone was staring, crying, or sobbing as the fire burned down toward its dying ashes.

Remembering that adhesive tape strewn on the Reverend's floor reminded Hardrock of a large roll of duct tape in the equipment locker in the gym, and he hurried there on his way to Burt Mines.

There are many accounts of what happened next. Here is the actual trial record in the safe at the Free Fall police department. Most of the participants are alive today, making accuracy in reporting even more important.

Hardrock cruised past the Mine Headquarters building and continued south toward the mine-mouth. In sight of the glow from lights at the mine-mouth, he switched off his headlights and began slowing. Suddenly ahead in the mine-mouth parking lot four men were standing and laughing toward the tipple, where the tipple operator was dangling a man rather than coal in the tipple shovel. One of the four men on the gravel and slag parking lot was Rodney Burt, Sr., accompanied by two men in suits and hats, and a fourth in miner's gear.

With approximately a hundred feet to go Hardrock mashed his accelerator, heading straight toward them and reaching them approximately 13 seconds after his fateful decision. It took the four men about 12 seconds to leave their standing positions. Rodney Burt and one of his guards, Rick Blades, to the right, and Joe Crouch and the miner known as Slim at the mountain church, crunching gravel and slag when they rose, and again when they landed. Like the parting of the waves, a witness later described it. And the next four or five seconds for Hardrock to screech his brakes, leap from his car, and give added directions.

"I'll bet you're Rick Blades," Hardrock called to one of the two brawny suited men, earlier also wearing a hat, and as the man responded by rolling toward a more upright position Hardrock met his rising chin with a descending right, at the same time borrowing his .45.

"Stay down," he cried. "Everybody. Or I'll knock you down."

Of the four men adorning the parking lot the miner nicknamed Slim seemed to recognize him first. At least he acted in terms of clearing his weapon from his holster. Rather than shoot him "like a dog on the ground" Hardrock leaped to him and reshaped his jaw in the same motion. It might or might not be only temporary. Rick Blades and Joe Crouch, the two thugs wearing suits and at one point hats, followed typically, grabbing for whatever as they rolled across gravel and slag. Rodney Burt, Sr., looked amazed that this could be happening to him.

Hardrock exercised his borrowed weapon—after all, the bullets were free—firing close enough to the two hatless heads to assure their owners' prompt attention. Rodney Burt himself, primarily on his back but with his right arm reaching, now flashed his weapon. Hardrock reached Rodney with his long left, and as the latter sprawled back softly against the hard surface Hardrock fired a final warning shot for all four, raced past his car, and aimed his weapon at the tipple operator a half dozen coal-car lengths beyond. "Down!" he yelled.

Hardrock's car in halting had skidded aside, hiding him for the most part from the operator but also hiding the operator from him. Now he stared for a moment at the operator—Buckshot Burt himself, heir to the Burt dynasty. And being whipped about in the tipple shovel above Buckshot was some poor miner for whatever reason. Buckshot's hand also found his weapon, obviously a habit with at least important personnel at Burt Mines. After glancing behind him at his four prone prisoners, Hardrock sprang toward the operator. The latter changed from operator to receiver as Hardrock's right just managed to reach high enough. Buckshot rolled off the tipple seat as if from a diving board across the Mighty Risky.

"I have him," Hardrock called to the badly shaken miner. "You're coming down." Movement of several levers soon activated the shovel in a downward direction. As the miner descended, Hardrock gave his five prisoners a quick glance. Buckshot's hand was moving like a snake on a slippery surface, gliding across rough gravel and slag, obviously grasping for his beleaguered weapon. Hardrock fired once, shattering enough of the weapon to disappoint gun lovers including Rodney Burt, Sr., for the life of the gun. "The next time I'll hit gun owners," Hardrock called, and to the suspended miner staggering from the tipple shovel he added, "We're home free."

The miner turned. "I'm tying him to that shovel. Higher than me. See if *he* makes it."

"No," Hardrock said. "Getting even may not be an answer after all."

"I plan to get even."

"Well, meanwhile you can help me get them locked up. I've got some wrapping tape in the car. Made for their wrists."

"That's just the first step," the miner said hurrying on that mission.

Hardrock swung his gun around to show "oneness" with his five downed prisoners. "Anyone moves, it's final," he warned. "They probably wouldn't yell out but they might," he explained as the miner returned with an armful of tape. "Would you swap this gun for that?"

"Can't wait."

"I know you have your reasons, but don't fire unless they move."

"Yes, except I count breathing as moving."

Hardrock laughed briefly and with his handfuls of tape surveyed his prisoners. "All right, one at a time. Everybody's hands behind their back, if you can hear me." Hardrock's laugh became less humorous. "If you can't, this gentleman here will make a hole where your ear's supposed to be." Hands began moving slowly but surely toward the owners' backs. Even Burt managed to maneuver his hands behind him, though in the process he seemed to cough out a mouthful of gravel and slag dust. Perhaps it tasted too much like imported cigars. Or perhaps smoke from the burning slag heap irritated his throat.

As Hardrock wrapped wrists, he was reminded of that much more pleasant visit with Amanda and her father at the swinging bridge. He laughed. "Excuse me a minute," he told the miner and strode near the office to a pickup labeled BURT

MINES. Hardrock lowered the truck's tailgate and unloaded its cargo of lighter cord, then backed the truck to the waiting five.

"Sir," he told the miner, "excuse me if I step in your way." At his car Hardrock brought out another roll of adhesive tape. "They probably wouldn't yell out, but they might," he explained. Then he began rolling the quintet over, one at a time, and as soon as someone faced skyward he stifled such cries as, "Hey, you Wholly Roller, that hurts." And, "you're next. You're dead." The tape stuck well. One had to feel reassured about Reverend Hope—almost always a good buyer of school supplies.

"I'll help you load 'em," the miner said.

"Good."

"All right, you can be first," Hardrock told Rick Blades, and as he grabbed Blades' right arm the miner's free hand grabbed his left. Blades' muscular torso made him a little difficult to handle, but Hardrock and the miner managed to heave him belly first onto the truck bed floor where, with a little scrambling of his knees, Rick avoided lying suspended where the tail gate could have been.

Hardrock nodded toward Buckshot next, a prisoner who promptly began receiving similar treatment in his awkward boarding of the pickup.

One leg was left, however. All five prisoners were aboard except the right leg of Rodney Burt, Sr. He had managed to squeeze his back onto the pickup bed, with his right leg remaining to dangle from the pickup like a burst exhaust pipe. Hardrock went to the aberrant leg and cradled it over the end of the truck. Then he eased it into a more comfortable position with its owner in the bed. Don't get mad, just get even. Or is it, he wondered, turn the other leg?

Or as his stepfather would say "make sure that leg is closed."

14

ROLL TIDE ROLL
All Over The Place

The fact that Hardrock single-handedly captured five men at Burt Mines is one of the best kept secrets in the Free Fall area. In a land that praises manhood, the capture of five men by one is a matter of shame.

Hardrock's reputation as a fighter grew steadily. His name was often associated with captor of unidentified Kentuckians and his fame grew.

When the University of Alabama promised Coach Saban $32,000,000 to leave Miami and come to Tuscaloosa, it was a gesture that also meant something to Hardrock Adams up in Free Fall, Kentucky. A $32,000,000 input into the economy of a relatively small city like Tuscaloosa would add some meat to some potatoes. In addition he heard somewhere that Coach Saban's wife was daughter of a coal miner in nearby West Virginia, which conceivably could help win over the coach. In addition a college-bound recent high school graduate had to start somewhere, and what was wrong with the University of Alabama, at least on par with most major universities. Travel was his future.

The school heard of Hardrock's need and loaned him an ancient Ford on "extended time." A graduating classmate heard of his plans and gave him a cap labeled ALABAMA.

Driving the Ford and wearing the cap he reached the interstate between Louisville and Nashville and took a hard left. Was he leaving Free Fall just as the going got rough? Target for Burt Mines? Warm their hands at the girls' dorm. Or shooting out a light over Brother Hope's head while he was speaking. Or Buckshot Burt writing him that nasty note at school and Amanda taking up for him. Or selling pornography in the neighborhood. Unqualified slum bums.

Suddenly Hardrock turned his Alabama cap to backwards, showing his scorn for all those challenges. He wasn't dodging them. To them, yes. But away, no. He returned his cap to its normal position. Forsaken, maybe. But not forgotten.

In Tuscaloosa he eased into the busy parking lot at a sports store. A large sign greeted Hardrock with the words "BOOKSTORE. I LOVE ALABAMA." It seemed an appropriate welcome, and Hardrock parked in its lot. In the store he found a half dozen customers, four of them near the cashier. One of them, of possible right guard heritage, told the cashier, "Things ain't like they used to be, and that's for sure."

"How's that, sir?"

The speaker appeared not to hear.

"How's that, sir?" the cashier repeated.

The man turned toward the others with a laugh. "She don't remember no Bear, or if she had she'd heard the first time?"

"She'd know him if she ever met him," assured the only female member of the group. "He said, 'Settling for a tie is like kissing your sister.'"

"Or whichever," interjected the first speaker.

"How about the new coach?" Hardrock asked the counter top. "He doesn't sound like he believes in ties either."

"Who could imagine kissing an Auburn woman anyway?" the guard asked.

There was general laughter as Hardrock nodded "Thanks" to the cashier and turned to leave.

The one who entered first, who looked like he had played too long without a helmet, told the cashier, "I reckon you can sell me three more of them Alabama schedules if you got to."

The female member interjected, "I need two more myself. I already got two. That'll make four."

The guard laughed. "Bring it on. I need some and then some. That's why I'm here."

"That sounds like an interesting book," Hardrock said. He asked the cashier, "How much are they?"

"Seven ninety-five." She indicated the top book, entitled simply CRIMSON TIDE FOOTBALL, on a stack beside her register and handed Hardrock one for inspection. He turned to the page entitled, "Alabama's 2009 Football Schedule against All Opponents." The schedule touted Virginia Tech, Florida International, North Texas, Arkansas, Kentucky, Mississippi, South Carolina, Tennessee, LSU, Tennessee-Chattanooga, and Auburn. At the end of the list of opponents was a column called "Crimson Tide Score." But there was no similar column for the opponent's score.

"Don't we keep track of other people's scores?" Hardrock asked.

There was a general laughter. "What scores?" the woman asked.

Hardrock handed the cashier the book. "Seven ninety-five might be the difference between a meal and no meal at the university."

But when he declined the book he felt guilty. He came from a writing background. His stepfather was writing a history of snake-handling churches. His mother was poet and English teacher at Mountainside. He believed what he was hearing about the megabucks at the Crimson Tide. "I'll buy that Crimson Tide book after all," he said. Regardless of his tight budget, surely he could afford a winner.

He was determined to learn more about the Crimson Tide. After classes he began dropping by the huge Bryant-Denny Stadium practice arena.

15

FROM BOOKS TO BALLS
Tuscaloosa The Chief

When Hardrock first arrived on the Alabama campus, football overshadowed everything facing him as he entered the campus area. University-oriented sports stores greeted his approach. An older man, perhaps a professor, directed him to the Registration Building, and after squeezing into a distant parking space he registered. Though the pre-registration forms completed at Free Fall had somewhat prepared him, the actual costs were staggering. The registration reminded him that by any stretch of the imagination he was poor. Was the university too huge a step? Speaking of money matters, his mother barely received minimum wage as a teacher at Mountainside. His father made considerably less than that as a mountain preacher, known for invisible collections.

He realized he could count on no help from home. If anything he should send money there if he could.

Hardrock's mother had asked him to check out the university's English and history sections in the libraries, her teaching at Mountainside and his majors here at the university. So about nine o'clock that first evening, almost as an after-thought, he walked from his dorm to the library. The library's sign touted itself open until ten, and he thought he must be late. Surrounded by silence, a lone girl about his age sat at a table, in the computer room. Books and papers and a laptop computer confronting her. As if to cap her scholarly appearance, eyeglasses added to her features.

Hardrock nodded aside to the library's other solitary female, the librarian, then came to the single, if dedicated girl student. "Please excuse my brief introduction," he said. "But it just occurred to me that we resemble two ships passing in the night."

She was so interested in reading something, she didn't hear his interruption.

"Sorry, I'm interrupting."

"What did you say?" She smiled. "I realize now that you said something."

"It was so brilliant I forgot what it was I said. Like two ships passing in the night. Where is everybody? Has the library closed?"

She laughed. "No. I guess it takes a few days of schooling to get people coming this way."

"So you're different?"

She smiled at him, "Apparently we're both different. Unless you're an employee. You are a student aren't you?"

"Yes, I'm Hardrock—that's correct—Hardrock Adams. As far as I know I'm majoring in history and creative writing. Subjects, of course, this library is made of."

"That's interesting. I'm also into history."

He glanced down at the nearest stack of documents. "Looks like something really does have your interest."

"On yes. I'm really interested. You should see inside my car. More books and pamphlets, including newspapers. I'm working on a history of Clarke County, Alabama."

"Clarke County, Alabama? Sounds interesting."

She put a hand on the nearer stack, almost as if caressing it. "I was born in a little town called Piney, Alabama. Right near Riser."

"Go ahead."

"Well, Riser is near Grove Hill, the county seat. Grove Hill was incorporated in the 1800's."

"Please. So all this is Clarke County history? By the way, you didn't tell me your name?"

"Ruth Moore."

"Are you going to write all this history yourself? You know, I claim to be a little bit of a writer myself. My mother teaches English and my stepfather writes history."

She laughed. "I'm not a writer, I'm a researcher. That's why I guess I just keep gathering material in the rough."

"If we're both here at closing time, do you mind if I help you take whatever to your car?"

She smiled. "I really wouldn't mind at all."

Nor did she. They unloaded her library material into her new car. "I really am grateful," she told him. "Shall I drive you to your car?"

"It's back at my dorm. Awhile ago it wouldn't start. But it's only a few blocks walk."

"I'm driving right by there."

"Well yes then. Which reminds me. I'll find out tomorrow, but I may have a job in the dining hall. Roughly four to eight. Do you plan to be at the library tomorrow evening again?"

"Oh yes. I'd be pleased to see you again."

"So be it," Hardrock said and meant it.

16

PAYBACK
Bloodline

The next evening when Ruth returned to the library she revealed a surprising background. A classmate awarded them with his presence. His eyes toward Ruth, his left hand feeling blindly for Hardrock, he said, "Ruth, I'm glad I met you."

Hardrock met his groping left hand, "Hardrock Adams," Hardrock said.

"Ruth, I'm glad I'm here," the new newcomer said, talking past Hardrock. For some strange reason he reminded Hardrock of Buckshot Burt, son of mine owner Rodney Burt and Hardrock's longtime adversary dating back to grade school days, Hardrock dismissed the groping hand.

The energetic newcomer said, "Ruth, that movie you've been waiting for has finally hit Tuscaloosa. How does ten o'clock tonight sound?"

"Hardrock," Ruth said, "this is Gene Cooper. Hardrock, Gene. That does sound interesting."

Hardrock surprised the newcomer with a hand-shake. "How are you?"

"Yes," the visitor replied without enthusiasm, "Gene Cooper."

Ruth laughed. "I forgot. I did promise to go. Do we leave now?"

"Yes." Cooper faced Hardrock. "You're welcome to join us. Some of the picture was made in Tuscaloosa."

"Thanks anyway," Hardrock said. "I'll see you later," he told Ruth. "Have fun."

"Why not? Go Alabama," Ruth said as lightly, trailing Cooper from the room as if meant to be.

Ruth was already in the computer room when Hardrock returned to the conversation that had ended so abruptly the previous evening.

"I hope you enjoyed your movie," he greeted her.

"Yes indeed," she said. "Sorry you missed it."

"Your Clarke County history. Still working on it?"

She laughed. "At this point I'm not sure. But yes."

"Mind if I join you? Unless you're expecting Gene again."

"Please do. I'm not sure when, or even if, he's coming by. It depends on his poker games."

Hardrock almost held his chair in mid-air before

sitting on it. "Poker?"

"Yes, at the off-campus poker house."

"Do they give degrees?"

She laughed. "If they do, Gene Cooper will be the first to get one. He'll tell you. A house full of poker players. And if they're not being raided they'll smoke pot."

He glanced toward a sheet of paper entitled MEALS ON WHEELS. "Excuse me," he said. "I can't help but notice. Did they have Meals on Wheels back in Clarke County history or Pickett's history?"

"It's just to remind me to check out potential clients. I'm in the process of organizing in Tuscaloosa. The state's largest city, Birmingham, has an outstanding program. It occurred to me that Tuscaloosa qualifies just as strongly, and that I should do something good ever since my fiancé was killed in a car crash. So I decided to squeeze Meals On Wheels into my schedule."

"That accident must have been terrible," Hardrock said.

"It was the worst."

"Are your parents proud of their daughter?"

"My parents are part of the problem. In Clarke County I was writing a chapter on wages and discovered, to my dismay, that my parents have constantly paid below the minimum wage to help around the house, and I'm sure for the pine industry."

"So you're trying to make amends. Any way I can help?"

She gave him a quick look, "You mean you'd like to go along to call on applicants?"

"Unless I'd be in the way? Tell me about it," he said.

Her expression was one of pleasure, not of triumph.

"Well, this potential client is older and has a long white beard. He cares for his invalid grand-daughter. He has an unpainted house behind a yard and porch, both sagging. For some reason the back door is nailed shut. Which doesn't help Meals On Wheels. I need to drive out there this evening to make sure he qualifies. So how to get food trays from the street into the house? This client says he knows his own front yard and porch and can accept his food tray at the street. Because some of our food carriers are also elderly and might trip if they brought the trays across the yard and porch. Too confusing?"

"Understood," Hardrock said. "Do you want me to drive?"

"Maybe later," she said, "I've been there once before."

They left the library with Ruth driving.

"It won't take long," she reassured him.

He didn't miss his Ford back at the dorm. In fact it would have been hard to explain anything more complete than this big pride from General Motors.

"No reason for both of us to slip," she said, "I can see him by myself."

"If we fall, we'll fall together," he said.

They held each other's hand and made it. The man with the long white beard responded promptly.

"Here's your acceptance form," Ruth said. "We'll park at your lot every day near noon, Monday through Friday. Is that clear?"

"Yes'm."

"Well, thank you," Ruth said. "The best of luck."

"Yes'm."

They returned to the car.

Hardrock said, "I don't see how it could be much tougher."

"Slanted front porch, back door locked and nailed shut," she agreed.

Ruth said, "This next potential client is on the opposite side of town. Instead of a nice old gentleman caring for his grandchild, it is an elderly couple replaying Tuscaloosa's role in the Old South. By the way, if you'd like to drive you're welcome to."

"If you insist," Hardrock said with a grin and headed around to the driver's side of the car. "You said the Old South?" he added.

"Yes. Turn back at the country store and head back into south Tuscaloosa."

This drive took them through downtown

Tuscaloosa. They were passing landmarks—Bryant-Denny Stadium, the Hotel Capstone, Interstate Highway 82 South.

Ruth said, "They live in a large two-story house with a second story balcony over a curved driveway."

"Sounds impressive."

"It is. The only thing is, as the cost of upkeep on the house increased, the family income decreased."

"Why didn't they move?"

"You'll see why. They started opening their home on evenings and weekends. Neighbors accused the Roberts of reopening the Civil War—make that the War Between the States. They still feel that the South shall rise again."

"Well leave me out of that one," Hardrock said. "I'm from Kentucky, maybe too far North."

"Not to me," Ruth said. "Since I met you, I've started thinking about 'Meals on Wheels' in Harlan County, Kentucky."

"It's not like going to Birmingham," Hardrock said, "But it's a step in the right direction."

"Good luck."

On this note of promise they approached the Old South.

"You should be able to see them now through the trees."

"That house is enough for me."

"They live the parts. They claim that when the

War Between the States ended they lost all their regular income and had to run a museum to survive."

"Well they survived all right. Looks like they are modeling Confederate clothes. A little tight at the corners."

"He helps you park your car in case there's a traffic problem – which there isn't."

Ruth smiled as they parked at the prospective couples.

"If you'll please pass the front door so other people can join us," the proprietor told her. They parked off to the side where he pointed, as Hardrock at last emerged from her car. In addition to his tight uniform the proprietor's medals indicated that he was a general.

"Welcome aboard," he said to his visitors.

"I'm Sophie Edwards," the hostess said, wearing an antebellum bonnet over an otherwise trim dress, "I guess I told you that my husband's name is Joel. We operate the Civil War Museum Between the States."

"I'm Hardrock Adams, pleased to meet you," Hardrock said.

Ruth said, "And here's your completed Meals On Wheels application form."

"Come in before the next people get here," Joel interrupted, accepting the paper. Joel nodded to Sophie who quickly opened the front door.

They soon found themselves in the entrance to

a massive living room seemingly covered by photographs and captions. Everyone wore some kind of Confederate uniform. Joel Edwards gestured toward the panorama. "What you see is what you get," he said glibly.

"Impressive," Hardrock said, "a hundred thousand fans all witnessing a life and death struggle. Impressive."

"Amen," Joel said with enthusiasm.

Hardrock added, "It reminds me of a football stadium," and hoped that his observation made sense. "Your household, a hundred thousand activists, the life and death struggle."

"Amen," Joel said again with enthusiasm. "In fact, if we'd had Coach Nick Saban we'd have won that war."

"One thing more," Hardrock said, pushing his luck. "What's that horseshoe doing upside down surrounded by all the stars way down at the far end of your living room?"

Joel caught the pass and began traveling, "Our boys were late with the message, communication being what it was. When nighttime came we should have moved. We'd of done it at home. The orders were for General Beauregard to advance before dawn. He never got the message. It is a known fact that Confederate soldiers are much more comfortable with night time forays than the Union troops. To win a battle like this would win the war."

"Joel," his wife interrupted, her impatience at last overcoming her decorum, "he didn't want a full battle report."

"I have seven that were giveaways like that."

As the four turned to leave, Sophie glanced at her dedicated husband. Awkwardly he backed to the front door and eased it open. There appeared a five gallon pail bluntly labeled COLLECTION.

Joel flushed slightly, and then eased back into line.

Ruth was next to respond. She laughed slightly, "Oh, I almost forgot." From her trim purse she pulled a fifty dollar bill and dropped it in the pail. Hardrock in a state of semi-shock was observing the bill. He couldn't remember ever having seen one. In fact, it occurred to him that you could buy Free Fall with it. But as he debated how to apply his billfold, his fingers found help.

"Thanks much," Ruth told the Edwards. "That was for both of us."

17

JUST CALL ME MISTER
As Well As The Other

The next evening they worked on the Clarke County history, checking document titles with library stock, all coordinated by the laptop. But as they worked with library material Hardrock found himself interested in books about the Crimson Tide. Ruth said, "By the way, I was clicking the A's awhile ago on my laptop and there isn't an updated book about Alabama football. But it also doesn't have one about the mighty Auburn."

"Oh boy," Hardrock said. "Even up in the Appalachians we understand you can't have one without the other."

She laughed. "Don't tell my parents, but I like Auburn like I like the Tide. Loveliest village on the plains. War eagle. Of course, they didn't have the hard cash, or didn't use what they had, to pay a coach in megabucks. But don't tell that to the players. Or to the fans either."

"For some reason I heard about the Crimson Tide and not War Eagle," Hardrock said, "but anyway, how's Clarke County doing?"

"Picket's history is the best overall coverage of early Alabama history," she said, "as you may know. I've ordered a copy from the rare books dealer."

"The library has a copy," he said. "I just saw it in an index. A rare book edition might cost thirty or forty dollars."

"Oh, I don't mind. I like to underline."

It was when he was helping her take her material to her car that Friday evening that he had his first real rude awakening.

"You've changed cars," he said. A long white Cadillac awaited them.

She laughed. "I have two cars. I drive the other one here in Tuscaloosa. And I take this one when I drive to Riser. I'm supposed to drive there tomorrow. Would you like to visit the county we're studying about?"

"I sure would. I don't have to work tomorrow. But..." He glanced uncertainly toward the new car. "Transportation?"

She laughed. "Right here it is. My father would have a heart attack if I came home in something else."

"If I can help in someway, I'll be glad to."

It was the most pleasant ride Hardrock could remember. In fact it was even more pleasant than when he captured those five Kentuckians. They reached Ruth's house and things went smoothly also. Including a last minute shopping visit by Ruth and her mother.

C. D. and Hardrock visited in the luxurious living room.

"Ruth will be back soon," her father reassured Hardrock. "She was helping her mother with some quick shopping."

"Right," Hardrock said.

"Your offer to help her with her history sounds good. She started that history thing in high school, believe it or not. Then she met this boy and they almost married but a month before their wedding he dies in a car wreck."

Hardrock looked silently at C.D. The latter, a large man, exhaled a loud breath. "I'll get right to the point, Mr. Adams. To my wife Sue and me, Ruth is the apple of our eyes. Anything that makes her happy makes us happy. We appreciate your helping in the library and driving her down here, even if it is my car, and talking all that stuff about history."

"I'm Hardrock, Mr. Moore. That really is my first name. Yes, I really am interested in the Clarke County history. My mother, who teaches in a Kentucky mountain school, is an outstanding poet, and I guess you could say has interested me in the written word."

"Ruth has always liked writing, too, I reckon. There's not much expense in doing a book. She's welcome to work out as she likes. You an Alabama fan?"

"State of Alabama?"

He laughed briefly. "No. Everybody's a state of Alabama fan. I mean state of Alabama football. The great and only everlasting Crimson Tide."

"Sure. I stopped at a store as I drove into Tuscaloosa earlier this week. They were selling an Alabama football book that didn't have a place for anybody else's score. I like that. I'm thinking of maybe putting in something selling sports books."

A lull followed.

Hardrock said, "With Ruth and her mother away for a little wonder if I shouldn't stroll around town. Ruth has described Riser so much it sounds fascinating."

"Certainly," C.D. agreed. "Drive around if you'd like. I'm here for a phone call. Would you rather drive?"

"No thanks. I'll walk. Bring you anything?"

C.D. grinned. "Maybe a good report."

Hardrock recognized the famed cotton mill once flourishing almost squarely in the middle of town. Next the train depot, now a shadow of its "Old South". Beside the tracks the boarding house once strictly reserved for whites. At a garage between the tracks and Main Street a man loitered and Hardrock joined him. "Hello, sir. Do you know a family named the C.D. Moores?"

"I know Mr. Moore best. Or know about him. Richest man in these parts. Ten thousand acres of growing pines I hear. Claims he is doing it by a domino theory."

"Domino theory?"

"That's right. Buys forty acres of trees. Then from selling the trees, or borrowing on them, gets enough money to buy a forty next door. Anybody can do it. He sure has."

"He seems sharp all right. A real Alabama fan."

"To the core. They tell me they don't make a move at the university he doesn't stack up and tie with a string."

"That's interesting. Speaking of Bama, apparently they're getting a good coach."

"They'd better have. Thirty-two million, there's no way but straight ahead."

"Well go, Bama," Hardrock concluded. "Have a good day."

"Same to you, sir. Have it and then some."

Back at the house, C.D. still in his rocker was studying a land map. "A good report?" he asked as Hardrock entered.

"Absolutely. At a garage near the depot I of course met another Crimson Tide fan. Which reminds me of another question. As a good businessman, what do you think of my publishing an Alabama football history? Maybe selling with a history of course of Clarke County?"

C.D.'s face resembled a good poker player's. "Of course I don't know anything about that. Except maybe books are made from trees."

"Not from an experience point of view but from a business point of view. Bama pays top money in the nation for a coach. He hires a staff that resembles the Magna Carte. It's knee-jerk time with everybody. At the first Tuscaloosa store, I met a half dozen people crowding the cash register to buy a little flimsy $7.95 book containing Alabama's football schedule without a place for opposing scores. Talk about a Christmas item."

"First," C.D. said, "let's see how we do with that little Clarke County history, okay, son? Okay?"

That first visit in Riser gave Hardrock a new sense of values. Hardrock considered himself just one step higher than a homeless person, maybe one step higher than the poverty level. At Mountainside money was as scarce as alcohol. His mother's poverty at Mountainside, or almost – and his father's meager church collections – were awesome. He couldn't remember ever getting anything without debating its cost. And now he was in the ballpark with a girl his own age, interested in the same kind of studies, attractive, and intelligent, a girl from the Old South as he envisioned a girl from the Old South, on the rebound from a tragedy, and yet driving a flashy Cadillac and whose father owned 10,000 acres maybe just for starters, at the minimum a millionaire. Almost everything that happened between them had tested their different social differences.

As for love, what was that? Was it more for who she was, or for starters more for what she had? The only way he'd learned to escape poverty was to work at something. And that something wasn't coal mining. The only part-time employment when attending Mountainside was to work at the school or a local mine. The mine you could have, and part-time work at the school was minimal. The school had swapped him the aged Ford for some part-time employment in its athletic department, and now this vehicle apparently was about to drop in the road.

The university dining hall would at least be minimum wage. And at least he knew something about writing. He had some things he had written that had never been picked up that should make his creative writing course take less time. Along with helping Ruth with her history maybe at that he could put together enough pages about Alabama football to make an interesting history.

Weekday evenings he and Ruth continued meeting at the library interspersed with their Riser trips as they worked on their combined projects. Apart from the cost, eating out in Tuscaloosa didn't seem appropriate when one of them made a living working in a dining hall.

They set a book publishing deadline of early

2010, hopefully for both books, finishing the Clarke history on time and only a month late with the Alabama football history. They made 15 copies of the county history, the first one going to the University of Alabama library. Hardrock, almost as an afterthought, talked a leading Tuscaloosa printer into doing 2,000 Crimson Tide books on credit, waiting to get paid until the books sold. The printer said that printers almost never fall for this arrangement with authors but in this case – in honor of Coach Saban – he would. Hardrock increased his initial request to 3,000 copies, and the printer – again presumably in honor of Coach Saban – agreed. He and Hardrock shook hands before Hardrock left, the printer adding, "Roll Tide, roll."

For the opening game of Alabama's 2010 season Hardrock planned to run ads in the Tuscaloosa News asking students to sell copies to fans entering and departing the great stadium. Meanwhile, Hardrock asked Ruth if she thought it appropriate to cap their projects' completion with their marriage. She thought it over for about a minute and then decided that it could be.

C.D. and Sue Moore considered a complete wedding extravaganza but then decided that the memory of the death of Ruth's former fiancé was a factor. So C.D. phoned an attorney in Mississippi who arranged for a wedding license and a marriage ceremony by a former Riser rector. As a wedding gift C.D. and Sue gave them a honeymoon trip to the Bahamas. When they returned from a fabulous and extended voyage, her parents gave a widely-attended reception. Among other small and large talk, one attendee was heard to remark, "I didn't know she married a Yankee."

Ruth and Hardrock approached their honeymoon with the festivity of youngsters. At their door they halted as if from common impulse.

"Here's to Riser," Hardrock declared.

"Free Fall forever," Ruth exclaimed.

Back at the university, would-be subcontractors, Jerry Barnes and Jud Applegate found themselves in need of Yankee ingenuity. The mother firm in Birmingham was demanding immediate strategy. "I can see it now." Jud said, "This proposal they can't turn down. We grab hold of a bunch of old – maybe even wrecked – cars. We park them all around the athletic dorm. When those SEC yahoos come poking around for players making megabucks they see poverty row."

"Jud!" Jeff exclaimed. "Finally you've got something. We could start with a requisition for Hardrock Adams' old blue Ford now that he's driving around in a big white Cadillac."

18

THE ARENA
Champion

Hardrock had several reasons to be interested in the University. Of course his mother had that "feeling" that the Rolling Tide was in his future. The bookstore "free for all" without the opponents' scores. And then, Ruth's family background of backing the Crimson Tide.

Though Mountainside had no football team, Hardrock's background did include football. His stepfather, the Reverend Henry Boost, had written an unpublished manuscript entitled HOW TO WIN AT FOOTBALL. He had also written THE HISTORY OF SNAKE HANDLING IN AMERICAN CHURCHES, also unpublished. In his football manuscript he recommended going to Japan and recruiting 400-pound Samurai wrestlers for the offensive line. You could teach them English by using sign language. Hardrock had spent many a pleasant time in childhood tossing limbs and other debris into the Mighty Risky River. This reminded him of football.

It cost nothing to visit practices but Hardrock refused this as a reason for interest. At the stadium he was surprised by the variety of exercises being practiced individually or in groups. Hardrock felt proud as if in the presence of greatness. His thoughts returned to earth, however, as a football came sailing from its many companions and bounded to a stop on the sidelines near him. Hardrock fought off an impulse to claim it and toss it back into the action. But two days later it so happened another football left the flock and landed even closer. There was no one around so Hardrock decided it was time for his own action. He ran to the ball. Straightening, he sent it soaring to a distant figure. Shades of the Mighty Risky River... An assistant coach broke from his companions and strode toward Hardrock.

"Mighty good throw," the coach said.

"I tried."

"You play football?"

"I don't know anything except passing."

"Passing's a good word," the coach said and was gone. But when the coach returned to the group of coaches he said something to Coach Saban, and Hardrock thought that Saban glanced briefly in his direction.

Hardrock had completed a dozen or so visits to the practice arena when on another occasion the same assistant coach greeted him on the sidelines. The coach, like football, was short and to the point. "We have a uniform for you in the locker room. See if it fits."

Hardrock blinked. "What did you say?"

"We want to see you in a uniform."

"Sure," Hardrock said, "Maybe make a picture?"

His benefactor laughed only briefly. He was already leading the way.

The uniform seemed to help his throwing ability. He thought he caught Coach Saban's glance as he threw.

It is said that Nero fiddled while Rome burned. The opposite can be said of the University of Alabama athletic program. The department strengthened while the University looked in vain for some of those benefactors who had promised but not provided. One such elusive benefactor was C. D. Moore. C. D. Moore was father of Hardrock's wife Ruth.

A seat on the fifty yard line, just the right distance up, means that without question you're different. Not only are you in the best position to follow the game, some yahoo who has never been in a classroom can't jump up and down in front of your eyes. Hardrock with his three new in-laws sat in the coveted box, Hardrock on the left, then Ruth, then Mrs. Moore and then – you'd better believe – his eminence C.D. Moore. C.D. had announced this morning a half-million-endowment from C.D. to the University of Alabama with details being worked out.

Performing for them, out on the field, was another step toward a national championship.

Everything was as it should be. The crowds roared and sang and sang and roared, and the game hadn't even started. The Alabama Crimson Tide. Bright red. The color of blood. Not your own, of course. Oversized players. Megabucks coaching. Alabama's "Million Dollar Band"—Million dollars yes—played fearlessly.

At the coveted special box, high up on the fifty-yard line, Hardrock thought of his favorite poem, recited in class back at Mountainside School. "The Charge of the Light Brigade" by Alfred, Lord Tennyson.

CHARGE OF THE LIGHT BRIGADE

Cannon to the Left of Them
Cannon to the Right of Them
Volleyed and Thundered
Into the Jaws of Death
Into the Mouth of Hell
Rode the Six Hundred

Except that there was nothing light about the

Alabama team. The front line averaged 275 pounds. The players indeed seemed ready to take on the jaws of death.

So the game erupted continuously from one end of the field to the other.

Approximately 100,000 fans screamed approval. A gap in the crowd still featured an upper-deck fifty-yard line reserved suite for the gentry. As they say, "Best seat in the house."

Down on the playing field the battle continued. One-sided or not, the moving crescendo.

Yes, everything was working. Except that Alabama was trailing by three points in the fourth quarter. The first-string quarterback had a cracked rib and the second-stringer a bad ankle.

Yes, everything was working except that.

After all, the injured quarterback was only one player in eleven. You don't lose a national championship just because your first-string quarterback is injured. Unless your second-string quarterback is injured in turn. And starts hobbling instead of running back and forth. The memory of "Mighty Risky" flashed in his mind near the end of the fourth quarter. "Excuse me," he said as he rose. He hurried down to the empty locker room. He went to the Number 66 jersey and changed. He went straight from the locker room to the Alabama bench. He caught the eye of an assistant coach and pointed to himself. The assistant spoke to Coach Saban.

There were two minutes left in the game when Hardrock trotted in. He promptly dropped a pass from center but he scooped up the football and shoveled it forward like he would a Free Fall tree limb. The surprised center turned around, caught the pass, and held on. But he was blindsided by opposing players and tossed it. Hardrock grabbed the ball—go, Alabama—and darted to his left only to have several players jump on the center who seemed less surprised as he caught it. As the opposing team went for the center, Hardrock glanced toward the Alabama bench. They motioned for a pass, and Hardrock decided to give it at least one more try. He faked another pass to the center but this time closed his eyes and threw it past, one might say, the river bend.

A Bama receiver welcomed the ball. That receiver pitched the ball to a Bama teammate, presumably someone who could run better. And he did. Zigzagging back and forth near the goal line and plunged into the endzone. Then suddenly it was over. Teammates rushed to gather around Hardrock. Then he began making his way into the throng. Bama players grabbed and hugged him, but he hurried up to his seat for the endowers.

Alabama would survive.

19

VICTORY PARTY
Celebration

C.D.'s foursome rode an hour north to the Birmingham club to join many celebrants including their hosts, parents of Ruth's best Riser friend, Eva Joyce. By the time C.D. and his entourage joined Eva and her parents at the club, the celebrants' orchestra was tossing music to the wind. "The Charge Of the Light Brigade" had been tame compared to this. The drummer—or drummers—there were two—seemed bent on at least one touchdown per stanza. Alabama's famed "Million Dollar Band" never sounded more earth- shattering than this music a short hour's drive from Tuscaloosa to Birmingham.

As patrons navigated back and forth to the bar or the musical fount itself, requesting drinks or tunes, it seemed that—genteel rich or no—jitterbugging on this occasion received equal billing with slower numbers. Riser's energetic Eva Joyce, for example, a self-styled "jitterbugging fool," appeared to be dancing with more partners than there were celebrants, all apparently eager to "go with the flow." Her husband tried weakly to maintain his place in line until alcohol helped him to a chair.

It definitely must be that Leroy Brown, "meanest man in the whole dang town," was "meaner than a junk yard dog." Unless "Mack The Knife" was himself in town.

Hardrock's dancing life in or around Free Fall had been limited. Dancing as well as drinking had been on Mountainside's hit list since the school's inception a century earlier. His mother had told him, "Talk about close. You can't put a knife between them when they're dancing." The few times he had slipped off with other students to a Fourth of July dance or similar, jitterbugging had far outnumbered slower dancing.

Tonight he and Ruth tried slower numbers mainly, Ruth leading slightly when necessary. After she and Hardrock had roughly made their way through the orchestra's slower numbers, Ruth suggested quietly that Hardrock might want to consider asking Eva to dance. He did and with Eva's expert guidance they made it all the way through "Jail House Rock." As they returned to their seats the orchestra blared off with "Rock

Around the Clock", and Eva looked at Ruth. "Do you mind, Ruth? He's a natural."

Ruth laughed. "Be my guest, Eva. I knew they practiced something in Free Fall."

"Do you mind?" Eva asked Hardrock.

He gave Ruth a quick grin and took Eva's hand.

Later, when he and Ruth were negotiating a slower dance, Ruth said, "Eva is really something isn't she?"

"She said, 'They call her jitterbug crazy.'"

"She isn't. Everyone really likes her. People want her to run for something in Riser, she's so outgoing and well-liked."

"Well she sure can jitterbug."

Outgoing such as at the Grand Old Opry in Nashville. Some Riser women travel somewhere each week, as they say, 'looking for culture', and Eva and some others decided to check out the Opry. As the crowd quieted one Saturday evening, Eva rose and announced to several thousand people, "We're from Riser, Alabama. You all come and visit us when you can." She was greeted by full-coverage applause.

"I could imagine," Hardrock said and could.

C.D. Moore's celebration was less joyful, no matter how tempting an overdose of free champagne and vodka. C.D.'s relative sobriety triggered an argument with a neighbor. "I'm positive our Alabama line totals more than half a ton. Averages—more than 300 pounds for each power ball Crimson Tide guy."

"No way, mister. They're either fast or heavy. They ain't both."

"I'm positive," C.D. managed to respond, a waiter interrupting.

As the evening roared on, with time a bewitching factor, celebrants prepared for the hay. Eva and her husband Ralph left for her parent's home near the club as C.D. and his group repaired to the Hyatt Hotel. It was agreed that C.D.'s group as well as Eva and her husband would awaken bright and early for their return trip to Riser. C.D.'s wife Sue, Sunday School President of the First Baptist Church of Riser, had been unable to get a substitute teacher, nor had Sunday school teacher Eva Joyce, both regulars attending the game. So they would try to reach Riser in time to salvage at least part of their stewardship.

20

REASONING TOGETHER
Both Brothers

The fact that Hardrock's mother and stepfather of Free Fall, Kentucky, attended the "REASONING" in Riser, Alabama, was by far the most talked about. As Hardrock's parents rode their family pickup south on Alabama Highway 58 their thoughts were ahead toward Pensacola, Florida, and the Gulf. They were heading for a conservative religious Pentecostal meeting featuring snake-handling. Some would call Brother Boost a conservative Pentecostalist. Afraid of reptiles in general, Hardrock's mother refused to glance back where a large rattlesnake rode the truck bed in a small cage.

It seemed miraculous that a highway sign read as it did, where it did: RISER, ALABAMA. SHORT WAY TO THE GULF. Included with Hardrock's last message and check home had been a chatty note that mentioned something about a bunch of public speakers. Wasn't that something today?

Brother Boost applied brakes as his wife said, "But remember, Henry, our room in Pensacola is paid for tonight."

The pickup stopped near Riser's Pensacola end. Traffic looked nil, and Henry made a U-turn in the four-lane street. Like his stepson, Hardrock, Henry took chances. He drove them back to a filling station. "I'm Reverend Boost," he told a lone youth. "I'm trying to find the C.D. Moore home."

"I can help. But they won't be there. Everybody in town is at the high school."

"And why is that, sir?" Brother Boost asked.

"Well, sir. People talking is what I heard."

"About what?"

"Go on three streets ahead and take a right. You can't miss it."

"I'd buy gas," Henry said. "But we filled it up at Greenville. Thanks." Henry remembered someone saying, "The Boosts are a polite family."

When they turned right, a long line of vehicles greeted them promptly.

It was a long walk, and Hardrock's mother decided to stay in the pickup. "If you'll bring Hardrock to me."

Eva Joyce surveyed the front entrance even as she chatted with well-wishers before the start of the Reasoning. A tall lanky middle-aged man arrived and slowed against the entering crowd. Something about the newcomer seemed familiar. She excused herself from her latest conversationalists and approached him. "May I help you, sir?" she asked him. "The program's almost starting."

He gave a bright smile, "You sure can, ma'am. I'm looking for my good-looking son, Hardrock Adams."

"You're what? I mean—."

"That's right. I'm Hardrock's stepdad. And I'll admit it."

She laughed. "That's reassuring. Anyway, he's one of the seven speakers on the platform." She indicated a panel of seven seated on the platform in front of a huge sign declaring COME LET US REASON TOGETHER SAYETH THE LORD. "Aren't you an Appalachian preacher?"

"I don't know about Appalachian. We do have trees growing out our ears."

"Then how about occupying the panelist's empty chair? We've been charging a hundred dollars a speaker, but to fill that empty chair I'll pay your way in."

"You're plucking the right strings. That's top billing."

"As you can guess by our sign, the topic is, 'Do we prefer diplomacy or do we prefer fighting?' We'd better run. They're going to start without us."

"Well I never met a preacher who turned down

an invite to speak," Brother Boost affirmed, heading for the platform.

Just then, outside the school building, an oversized truck bounced to a halt with a couple blasts of its horn. Eva squeezed outside again. Amazingly, it was a huge covered truck with a sign on its side: BROTHER ELFORD BOOST AND HIS DAUGHTER AMANDA. In the driver's seat Henry Boost swung open his truck door. Beside him sat his daughter, Amanda, with passenger Leroy on the far right.

Amazingly there were now two Boost trucks in this Alabama town: the pickup bearing Hardrock's mother and stepfather, Henry, and the large one bearing Brother Elford Boost and his daughter and husband. The famed Boost Brothers mix-up began abruptly. Eva had no sooner headed Henry Boost toward the panel than a cameraman for one of the visiting news agencies strayed dangerously in front of the arriving truck. The truck's horn, if not the truck itself, sought to establish eminent domain.

Reverend Elford Boost managed to squeeze his front bumper almost against the building's front door. "Never saw so much traffic in my life," he told all who would listen. "Anybody seen Miss Eva Joyce? Or I guess you could make that 'Mrs.'"

Eva, squeezed between inside and outside the building, managed a laugh and the faint remark, "I'm Eva."

"Well, your invitation got mixed up. I'm Elford and he's Henry."

Henry's shoulders drooped only slightly. "The Boost Brothers. Dig?"

Eva looked a little flustered. "Well somebody needs to come on stage." She resumed her leadership role toward the panel.

From behind the podium Eva announced, "Welcome, how welcome indeed. Yes, we have panelists here representing people throughout the United States. As you can see by the sign, our theme is, 'Come, let us reason together sayeth the Lord.' Shall we talk one-on-one or shall we fight one-on-one? The panelists, starting alphabetically from left to right, will each have ten minutes. I'll ring this bell when time is up. All right, may we have the first panelist please?"

But apparently this was not to be. Brother Boost himself rose fast as a Boost brother. "Please if I might, can I briefly interrupt? Folks, if you don't mind, I'd appreciate it if you'd let me be last. I just got here after driving my truck about five hundred miles in horn-blowing traffic, and I need to rearrange my smarts. I'm certainly not used to driving without Amanda. Anyways, my daughter, Amanda, got married and I'm still washing her name from my truck."

"Certainly, Reverend Boost," Eva agreed quickly. "I'm sure the other panelists agree. But first there's this minor correction. We had invited

Reverend Elford Boost to speak because of the well-known singing with his daughter. Instead the invitation went to Reverend Henry Boost, Reverend Elford's brother also in Free Fall. So in true reasoning manner we asked both of those gentlemen to meet with us today, but only Reverend Elford Boost will represent Free Fall. I trust this is clear."

There was a nodding of heads as she read a note of thanks from the National Democratic Party. "You may begin."

The young man coming to the podium looked surprisingly young.

"And now for our last panelist. Reverend Elford Boost of Free Fall, Kentucky." Eva's smile looked tentative, but there was nothing tentative about Brother Boost's speech.

"I'm Reverend Elford Boost, from Kentucky as the good lady says, near West Virginia as they say. My son has come all the way down here to marry a wonderful young lady in this home town. Anyway, I definitely do agree with this verse, of course, 'Come let us reason together sayeth the Lord.' And that same Lord was certainly the Prince of Peace, not of war. So much for the preliminaries."

"I myself am basically non-violent I guess you could say. Yet some might point out I come from one of the toughest histories in the United States. I come from a place known as, as the lady says, as Free Fall, Kentucky. Our county is Breathitt County known widely years ago as Bloody Breathitt. That was then, of course, not now. In World War I Breathitt and a county in Dakota had a hundred percent volunteers – highest in the nation. Alongside Breathitt some people looked like draft dodgers."

"In fact some time ago our school President had a death squad visit him, and if he hadn't said a cherry hello when they rode their horses in at daybreak, he'd long ago been Nellie bar the door. I'm telling this to show what talking things over can do. From talking things over, helped by a Christian Training School founded a century ago, we have become one of the most peaceful places on earth. My nephew Hardrock is a living example. Although not the most peaceful person in the world himself, he absolutely never goes out looking just for trouble. Amen."

"And, oh yes, one other thing, some of our teams up around Kentucky are themselves non-violent. If they weren't they might do a better job of taking on the Alabama Crimson Tide. Which my nephew, Hardrock, assures me is a topflight team again this year. Congratulations again and I thank you."

The scattering of applause following Reverend Boost's presentation became less scattered and more pronounced.

Hardrock was first to congratulate his stepfather after the panel discussion ended. "And where is Mom?" Hardrock asked. "And what are you doing in Riser, Alabama? But first, of course, Uncle, this is Ruth. Ruth, this is the father of 'Miss Appalachia'".

Brother Boost offered his hand. "Pleased to meet you, ma'am. And what a charming lady."

"Thank you. And say—"

"One thing at a time. Son, your mother's in the truck, as eager to see you as a homeless puppy. As for what we're doing here, we're headed for Pensacola, to a Pensacola get-together, and we saw the Riser sign. We're the farthest truck in that long line out there."

"My parents are here somewhere," Ruth said. "Hi, Mom and Dad."

"Most surely," Reverend Boost answered. "It's really wonderful to meet you, and we wish we could sit and talk a spell. But we need to reach Pensacola by nightfall. A good Pentecostal always walks in the light."

21

CHANGING OF THE GUARD
Attention

C. D. Moore lost the Riser, Alabama, mayoral race by 57 votes. He always said it was the first close race he'd ever lost. Two years after the race he died following a heart attack, and five months later Ruth's mother also died. C.D. willed Ruth seven million dollars. Oriented toward the Old South in which the male handles most of the business, she gave the seven million dollars to her husband, Hardrock Adams. But believing in the "golden means," Hardrock promptly split the difference, giving her back three-and-a-half million.

Hardrock's new wealth did not seem to go to his head. He rented a modest suite adjoining the Crimson Tide campus and in small letters had printed on the suite doorway OFFICE OF MOORE PUBLISHING COMPANY. People remember this

Crimson Tide fan in his early twenties seated in his modest office, tall yet not quite tall, dark yet not quite tanned, and handsome, a little bit more so. He hired a-half dozen students to work in the suite at almost double minimum wage. His parents remember those chatty letters he mailed along with checks.

Both Hardrock and Ruth found their studies at the university "easy going," partly because they were studying familiar subjects – Ruth in county research and Hardrock in sports history. Hardrock made frequent trips to the Crimson Tide football arena though never at the expense of the publishing company.

One less problem to worry about was, of all things, Burt Mines. Concomitant with his new wealth Hardrock formed the habit of reading the WALL STREET JOURNAL, now and then. One day he sat in his office with a store-to-store book salesman discussing the demographics of sports book readers. He opened to a JOURNAL page with a fascinating story about the suffering coal mine industry including the recent bankruptcy of the Burt Mines near Hazard, Kentucky.

"You wouldn't believe what that mine tried to do to that school," Hardrock informed the salesman. "On the other hand, as someone selling the truth you would."

No one realized he was sitting in the shade of three-and-a-half-million dollars except Ruth who had three-and-a-half millions for backup.

Though neither Ruth nor Hardrock seemed conceited because of their wealth, C.D.'s will itself bothered beneficiaries somewhat. For one thing, a number of blacks had worked in C.D.'s household for years and they were expecting at least a token bequest from his will. Except that C.D. was a believer in "keeping it in the family."

Hardrock and Ruth decided to help this situation by giving each former employee $2,000. Hardrock used the MOORE PUBLISHING COMPANY in mailing out the checks. He asked the student-receptionist to "call Riser until we have all the names and addresses."

"Yes sir, Mr. Adams. But, I wasn't clear. Do you want me to handle Mrs. Adams' mail out too?"

"Yes. For both of us please. We're combining our two checks."

"I have the addresses of a dozen churches for your tithe fund. Also the Mountainside School."

"That's good. Thanks."

"Reverend Hope, the President of Mountainside, called and asked if you'd be there for the dedication."

"They promised to send me pictures."

"Oh they did. They're on your desk."

He gave the receptionist a parting smile and hurried to his office. He opened the packet of photographs. The first was a panoramic photo of the old Burt Mines area. The second was a large marble sign that read DEDICATED. HARDROCK ADAMS CAMPUS. Formerly Burt Mines.